HEARING AND COMMUNICATION DISORDERS

A manual for CBR workers

•

Sheila Wirz

*Senior Lecturer, The National Hospital's
College of Speech Sciences, London*

and

Sandy Winyard

*Lecturer in Rehabilitation Studies,
University of Southampton*

150th YEAR
M
MACMILLAN

First published 1993

Published by THE MACMILLAN PRESS LTD
London and Basingstoke
Associated companies and representatives in Accra,
Auckland, Delhi, Dublin, Gaborone, Hamburg, Harare,
Hong Kong, Kuala Lumpur, Lagos, Manzini, Melbourne,
Mexico City, Nairobi, New York, Singapore, Tokyo.

ISBN 0–333–57448–6

Phototypeset by Intype, London
Printed in China

A catalogue record for this book is available from the
British Library.

Contents

iii

Preface

The ability to communicate effectively and efficiently has made it possible for the human race to develop and create cultures and civilisations in a diversity of ways not found in any other species in the animal kingdom. The development of speech and communication is a technical concern of the paediatrician, while the process of speech and hearing is also the concern of the ear, nose and throat specialist. However both depend heavily on the speech therapist for both detailed diagnosis of the communication problem and its subsequent management and treatment.

Unfortunately there are few speech therapists available and in many so-called developing countries there will be no more than one in each large city. During the 1970s health workers around the world came to understand the need for a large number of workers who could help with the thousands of disabled people who make up around 3 per cent of the population in every country.

As a result the concept of community based rehabilitation (CBR) was set up and the authors of this preface are proud to be amongst those who developed the first programme for training people in the concepts of community based rehabilitation in a university. For this course, many well experienced specialists were called in and we were particularly happy to have help from Sheila Wirz and Sandy Winyard who understood the enormous need for their knowledge and skills in developing countries. Although there is an excellent book *The Disabled Village Child* by David Werner, we knew of no specific book aimed at helping children with communication problems growing up in the countries of the south.

While this book is aimed particularly at CBR workers, it should also be useful to doctors and nurses concerned with primary health care, who will have had limited training in communication problems. It should be on the shelves of the libraries of every teacher-training college as it will help all teachers to understand the problems of some of the children with whom they have difficulty. This book is not one that can be just read through and put to one side. It demands that we observe communication, how it starts at birth, steadily develops and is very much more than speech. The book expects the reader to be involved with those with a variety of communication disorders so that direct observation can be made, and here the teacher or organiser has a responsibility to assist students in arranging and supervising the contacts and in creating the necessary discussion between students after such work.

We have no hesitation in strongly recommending this book to all those concerned to overcome the many communication problems that beset children and adults the world over.

Professor David Morley
Dr Pamela Zinkin

Acknowledgements

We would like to thank colleagues and course participants of the CBR Trainers and Planners Course at the Institute of Child Health, University of London, for helping us to shape our ideas for this book.

We would especially like to thank the Class of 91/92 who generously completed versions of the question sheets and helped us refine the questions.

Financial support for the publication of this book was generously provided by Interbrand Group plc, London

Introduction

This book is for Community Based Rehabilitation (CBR) workers and other health workers who work with disabled children. The book is about communication disorders in children and what can be done to help these children and their families.

All people communicate:

- it is how we make contact and make friends,
- it is how we operate in the family and in society,
- it is how we learn,
- it is how we make our needs and our interests known.

Babies, children, adults and old people all communicate. Sometimes these people use the same methods of communication, e.g. smiling, laughing and sometimes different methods, e.g. babies use crying but most adults do not communicate with crying very often.

Deaf people, cerebral palsied people, mentally handicapped people also all communicate. Sometimes they use the same form of communication as other people and sometimes they do not. Sometimes they have difficulty in understanding us and sometimes we have difficulty in understanding them.

This book is about communication with disabled people. It is arranged in Parts.

Communication is not just talking but a whole lot more as well. We need to understand what communication involves. **Part 1** of the book helps us to understand what communication involves and how it develops.

Section 1.1 is about aspects of communication and ensures that we all understand the same ideas about communication before we start understanding the rest of the book.

Babies learn to communicate with their mothers and families, **Section 1.2** of the book helps us to understand how communication develops.

Before we can begin to help children with communication disorders or their families we need to be able to observe communication. **Section 1.3** teaches us ways in which we can observe communication.

Some children fail to develop communication early. We need to understand what can go wrong with the development of communication. **Section 1.4** describes some of the ways in which communication may fail to develop.

We need to know how to help people with particular communication problems. **Part 2** refers to the communication problems of deaf people, **Part 3** to the problems of mentally handicapped children and **Part 4** to the problems of cerebral palsied children.

People who cannot communicate easily must not be teased. We need to develop awareness of communication disorder among the population. **Part 5** suggests ways in which we could do this.

Paediatricians (children's doctors) look at a child's communication when they are considering his development. ENT doctors (ear, nose and throat doctors) and teachers of the deaf consider the hearing and communication of deaf children. Speech therapists consider hearing and communication disorders for many different groups of people.

Where there is no teacher of the deaf or speech therapist or ENT doctor or paediatrician, CBR workers can do a lot to help these children.

CBR workers can:

- begin to identify the problem,
- send the child for further help when available,
- offer advice and help to the mother,
- help to prepare programmes for the family, and
- help the village teacher to take the child to school.

This book is not designed for speech therapists, for psychologists, for teachers of the deaf or for paediatricians who all understand something about communication disorder. **This book is for CBR workers** who during their work with disabled children and their families come across children with communication disorders. The children's communication disorders may occur alongside other difficulties or may occur alone.

The book has six parts.

Part 1   Introduction to communication
Part 2   Hearing and hearing loss
Part 3   Children with mental handicap (learning disorders)

Each of the sections has:

- a short **reading** explaining the issue,
- some suggestions of ways to develop **skills**, and
- **questions** at the end of each section to help you to see how much you have learned.

How to use this book

This book is designed to help people to understand something about the communication disorders of disabled children. As we have seen in the Introduction there are many people who are interested in communication disorders, e.g. paediatricians (children's doctors), ENT doctors (ear, nose and throat doctors), speech therapists (who know a lot about communication) and teachers of the deaf (who know about deaf children). This book is not designed for them. It is for Community Based Rehabilitation (CBR) and other health workers working with disabled children.

How do you learn?

We all learn in different ways e.g.:

- some people find it easiest to learn by reading something,
- others by watching other people,
- others by talking to people and
- others by trying things out.

This book uses all these ways of learning. It is not a textbook where you read the words but do not understand or remember anything after you have finished reading. The words in the book are not too difficult and we have tried to present the ideas in a simple form. Some of the ideas are not easy and readers will have to take time to think about what they have read.

Readers will need to be comfortable with their reading skills if they are to benefit from this book. Readers should as a minimum have completed elementary education or equivalent. The readings, questions and skills pages have been carefully designed and may not easily translate into your mother tongue or other languages, we therefore suggest that readers will need to have completed elementary education in English.

Will the book give me all the right answers?

No it will not. The book gives you lots of ideas about communication, communication disorders and what you might do to help the child/family but only the reader knows the special problems of *his* village, *that* child and *that* family. The book tries to develop your knowledge and skills about communication disorder but the reader will have to use his other knowledge and experience in applying this knowledge and skills.

Working alone or with a friend?

We suggest that readers will find it easier to use this book with a fellow CBR worker or as part of a training course because many of the skills exercises need two people. It is possible for someone to work through the book quite on their own but we feel to do this with a friend will be easier.

The order of reading the book

The sections are ordered in a particular way and **all readers should start with Part 1. Trainers can then choose whether to do Parts 2, 3 and 4 in a particular order but Part 1 must be read first**.

How to work through each section

You should first look at the readings of the section. These readings are not long and we have tried to make them clear. Read them carefully.

You should then talk about this with your friend and see if there are any words or ideas in the reading which you both do not fully understand. You should try to sort out any problems. You can then think about what you have read while you are gardening or cooking.

The next day you should try the questions without looking at the reading (or the answer sheet) to see how much you have understood and remembered.

You can then mark your answers using the answer sheets at the back of the book. If you have achieved 15 or more out of 20 marks on the answer sheet look at the reading again and see if you can understand why you did not get the right answer to some of the questions. Have the questions and your answers in front of you as you read the exercise again. Discuss any problems with your friend.

If you get less than 15 out of 20 on the questions, read the reading very carefully again, think about it and then try the questions again on a new sheet of paper.

When you have completed the questions to the exercise satisfactorily then try the skills section. Follow the instructions carefully and work where possible with your friend.

Do you need skills and knowledge?

Yes. We are quite sure that a CBR worker is able to work better if he/she understands **why** he/she is doing something.

The sections of this book are designed to develop both **skills** and **knowledge**. It is not good enough to concentrate on one or the other both must be developed. In addition a CBR worker needs to examine his **attitudes** to disability, to disabled people and to communication disorder.

Do you need specialist help?

Some CBR and health workers may work in settings where they can refer children with communication problems to a speech therapist or to an ENT doctor or to a school for the deaf. They are fortunate because they will be able to check with these people that their ideas as to what is wrong with the child are correct. They will also be able to plan a programme for the child with the help of the specialist. In such a situation the specialist will be able to help the CBR worker with the programme planning for the child and the CBR worker will be able to help the specialist by implementing the programme.

Other CBR workers work in settings where there are no specialists or very few specialists. The specialists may only be available in cities which are far away, expensive to reach and too far for regular help to be given. In such settings the CBR worker will be the specialist and will be the one who helps the family to help their child.

Both groups of CBR worker should find this book helpful. The book:

- introduces ideas about communication to the CBR worker,
- suggests ways in which the CBR worker can develop skills,
- gives question sheets for the reader to check his knowledge.

Do you have to go on a course?

Trainers and planners of CBR courses may find it useful to work through this book as the Hearing and Communication Module of their CBR training course. Trainers and planners should beware of concentrating only on the skills sections of the book. It is important that readers follow all parts of a section and that they follow the order of sections listed above.

PART 1

Introduction to Communication

SECTION 1.1

What is communication?

Human beings communicate with each other because they are social. When we think about communication, most people think about talking or speech, but, we communicate through a variety of methods. Talking, or speech, is just one of them. Here are some communicative methods:

- spoken language,
- listening,
- written language,
- pictures,
- by sounds,
- by smiling and laughing,
- by crying and frowning,
- by looking at each other,
- by touching,
- by gestures, and
- by facial expression.

Can you think of any more?

These methods of communication may be verbal or non-verbal. They may be for family communication or large group communication.

We communicate for a variety of reasons:

- to greet each other and acknowledge each others presence,
- to share information or emotions with people,
- to ask for something,
- to ask for something to be done,
- to explain things to someone,
- to answer Yes or No.

These are communicative functions.

Some communication is natural, in other words we are born with it, e.g. crying. Most babies cry as soon as they are born. We will see in the next section how babies learn to develop their cry into communication that means something. Babies learn other ways of communicating long before they can speak, e.g. looking at people, smiling, making sounds to people. However this learning to communicate only takes place in a social setting.

Some communication is learned in early childhood from the social setting the child spends his time in:

- his mother tongue language,
- sign language if his parents are deaf,
- the language of education, the official language of the country,
- later he will learn to read and write language.

Communication is two way. We express things by speech, writing, gesture, facial expression. We understand things by hearing, seeing, reading. We all express things and we all listen and understand what is being said to us.

Communication is two-way – everyone is a listener and a speaker

Communication allows a person to mix in his community and family. A person who cannot communicate early will be isolated, frustrated and find learning difficult. He might become aggressive and difficult and behave badly because he cannot make himself understood, or because he doesn't understand what is going on around him.

Listening is a very important aspect of communication. Listening is more than just hearing, it includes paying attention and making

One of these children is not listening

sense of what you hear and putting it together with the things you are seeing and feeling at the same time.

For most of us, verbal language is our main method of communication. Verbal language can be divided into a number of parts:

- voice,
- sounds,
- words,
- rules,
- intonation (the up and down of the voice).

Voice is the noise you make. When you scream or cry, you are using voice.

Sounds make up the words. Sounds are not always the same as the letters. **c a t** are the sounds for the word cat. **c a t** are the letters for the word cat. **s h o p** are the letters that spell shop, but **sh o p** are the sounds for shop.

So you say sounds and you write and spell letters.

Words carry the meaning of what you want to say. They carry the message.

Rules are used to put the words together. Each language has rules. For example, in English we put the colour of things before the word we are describing – green grass, blue sky, red ball. If we were speaking French, the colour comes after the word – grass green etc.

4

Intonation is the **melody** of speech, the ups and downs you hear in people's voices. The intonation can tell the listener a lot about the meaning of the words in the sentence, e.g. We're going out.

This sentence can be said as a question or as a statement, just by changing the intonation pattern. If it goes up at the end, it is a question. If it stays on the same level, it is a statement. Try it for yourselves.

These **language skills** are used for different functions (see page 2 of this section) e.g.:

- to ask questions,
- to share knowledge or information,
- as greetings,
- to express emotions or humour,
- to acknowledge people's presence or opinions etc.

We use verbal language together with non-verbal language to communicate.

Good communicators use lots of different methods of communication. Verbal language is just one method.

Good communicators use lots of different methods of communication

5

Questions

Section 1.1   What is communication?

1. Communication means just speech.   True/False   **Marks:**   1

2. A child who has no speech can   True/False   **Marks:**   1
    communicate.

3. Communication is a two-way process.   True/False   **Marks:**   1

4. The two-way process involves:
    a. expression/understanding,
    b. expression/talking.
    Choose a or b.   **Marks:**   1

5. Name four methods of communication   **Marks:**   4
    (four communicative methods).

6. Which of the methods you give in
    Question 5 are:
    • verbal
    • non-verbal.   **Marks:**   4

7. Name two reasons why people   **Marks:**   2
    communicate (two communicative
    functions).

8. List four parts of verbal language.   **Marks:**   4

9. Intonation helps us to understand   True/False   **Marks:**   1
    someone.

10. Sounds of words and letters of words are   True/False   **Marks:**   1
    the same.

Skills

Section 1.1   What is communication?

Activity 1

1. Observe a group of people talking.
    How are they communicating?
    Write down four communicative methods they are using.

2. Who in the group is expressing themselves?
    Who in the group is listening?
    Write down three ways a person is expressing themselves. (This will
    probably be a different list from answer 1.)

3. Observe the listeners.
   What are they doing?
   Write down three ways they are behaving.

4. Now look at your answer, and write down a list of communicative
   methods, under two headings:
   Listening and Expressing.
   Can you list six in each group?
   You may not have observed them all in 1 because the communication
   you observe will depend on the behaviour of the group.

Activity 2

Observe a baby with his mother.
What listening behaviours is the baby using?
What listening behaviours is the mother using?
What expressive behaviours is the mother using?
What expressive behaviours is the baby using?

Activity 3

1. Observe a small child with an adult.
   What communicative functions is the adult using?
   What communicative functions is the child using?

2. Is the small child using language and speech exactly as an adult?
   Does it matter, or does the adult understand him anyway?

Activity 4

Turn to the person sitting next to you or a friend and give him a message.
a. Using no voice: use your face, gestures, move your lips, write, use
   words, use language but no voice.
b. Using no words or language: make noises, gesture, use your face.
c. Using no facial expression.
d. Using no gestures.
e. Using only writing: no facial expression, gestures or words.
Ask your friend to say what methods of communication you are using.

SECTION 1.2

How does communication develop?

Early language development

Communication is a two-way (interactive) sharing process which begins at birth. The baby and whoever looks after her learn about each other and how to recognise the signals that each gives out.

These signals do not have to be **verbal** (using voice and speech). They can be **non-verbal** (eye-contact, gestures, facial expression, vocal – noises etc.), or a combination of both. For example wriggling and crying could mean:

- I'm hungry.
- I'm wet and uncomfortable.
- I want to be picked up and given some attention.

The way the caregiver responds to the signal the baby is giving out – in this case wriggling and crying – will influence the sort of wriggling and crying message the baby gives out next time.

Therefore if wriggling and crying in one way produces a change of nappy the baby will wriggle and cry in that way when she is wet and uncomfortable because she gets what she wants. If she is hungry she will try sending another signal to her caregiver, perhaps wriggle and cry in a different way. If the response from her caregiver is the right one – giving food to her – she will use the same signal again. If the response is not what the baby wants she will try sending a different signal until the caregiver responds correctly. The baby learns to change her communicative behaviour by the responses of the caregiver.

In this way the child and the caregiver learn to understand each other. They will change their signals and responses until they **fit together** – the signal gets the right response, meaning the message has been understood and both baby and caregiver are happy.

This is the beginning of turn-taking routines, which are the non-verbal framework for later verbal communication. When the baby is communicating the caregiver listens and when the caregiver communicates the baby stops what it is doing (kicking, crying, gurgling etc.) and listens and then will respond by crying, kicking, gurgling etc. and so the communication will continue, first one and then the other. Turn-taking is a very important part of communication.

The baby learns through her senses about the world in which she lives and how people communicate. She explores by hearing, touching, seeing, tasting and smelling and gradually comes to understand her environment.

By the end of her first year, the baby realises that she has some control over her caregiver's behaviour. She can use communicative signals as different communicative functions, e.g. certain gestures, vocalisations, eye contact, facial expression etc. and get things she wants. For example, a child sees a favourite toy on the top shelf,

A mother and baby communicating together

9

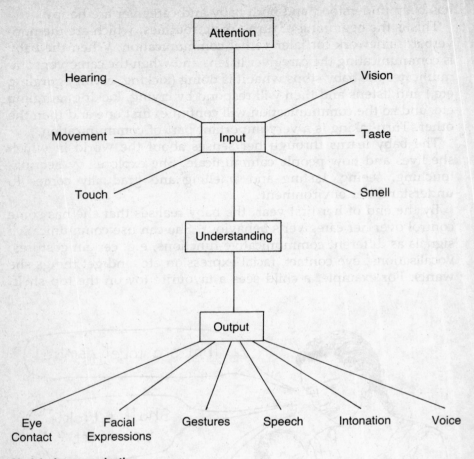

Model of communication

which she can't reach. She wants it, so she waves her arms around, makes noises, looks at her caregiver, looks at the toy, looks back at her caregiver. Her caregiver understands the message the baby is sending and gets the toy and gives it to her.

The same process applies when the baby wants to draw her mother's attention to something interesting, e.g. a dog barking or a noisy car or tractor.

This is **intentional behaviour**. The child is intending to send that particular message.

Speech sounds are added to this intentional behaviour and become more meaningful as the child copies adult intonation patterns (the melody or up and down of the voice in speech). This is called **jargon**. It is when the child seems to be talking to you,

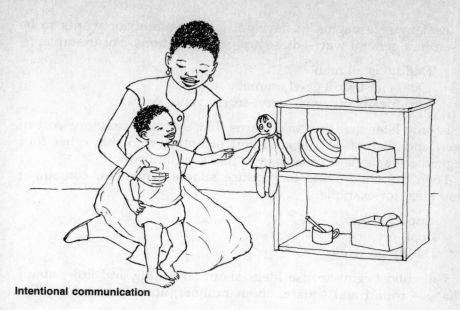

Intentional communication

because it sounds like adult speech, but you cannot recognise words. It is just melody and sounds.

It is this pattern of **turn taking, intentional communicating behaviour** and **jargon** that the baby develops in the first year.

First words develop from this framework and appear around 12–15 months. They allow the child to express a wider variety of intentions. The words will not appear if the baby has not developed the early framework.

Later language development

A child's first words are usually names of things around her that are important, e.g. Mummy, Daddy, cup, drink, swing, bed, cat etc. The child often uses and understands lots of different words before she starts putting them together.

When she does start to put two words together, they can often mean more than one thing and it is the way that she says them – the melody – and the general situation she is in that give the listener the clues he needs to understand the words correctly. For example, 'Mummy drink' could mean:

1. Mummy, I want a drink, or can I have a drink.
2. Mummy, here's my drink.
3. Mummy, do you want a drink?
4. Mummy, here's your drink.

As language begins to develop, it is common for words to be used in a general way – these are **generalisations**. For example:

'Daddy' is all men.
'Cat' is all four legged animals.
'Car' means car, bus, lorry, truck, van etc.

It is only later that the child learns that Daddy is only one sort of man and that cat is a special sort of animal and that other four legged animals have other names like goat and cow.

Then the child starts to produce **simple sentences**, containing one idea, for example:

Cup on floor.
Look my dolly.
Daddy go work.

The child begins to use ideas about size – big and little; about shape – round and square; about number; and about colour. For example:

The big ball is red.
My toy is big.
The blue brick is little.
There are four little cups.

Gradually the child will start to use more **complex sentences**, containing more than one idea. For example:

I want to play in the garden and have a drink.
My car is red and it is going to crash.

Normally children's language skills increase very quickly because they realise how useful it is, and how communicating with language can control other people and the conversation.

Children usually understand much more than they can say. This goes on being true when they grow up.

The child with normally developing language will often experience some difficulties with:

1. Making sounds correctly: e.g. saying 'tat' instead of 'cat', or 'date' instead of 'gate'.
2. Getting words in the right order: e.g. 'are we going by car home'.
3. Getting plurals and verb tenses right: e.g. 'mouses' instead of 'mice', 'sheeps' instead of 'sheep'; e.g. 'good, gooder, goodest' instead of 'good, better, best'; e.g. 'I wroted' or 'I writed' instead of 'I wrote'.

This is quite normal and will usually correct itself.

THE IMPORTANT POINT TO REMEMBER IS THAT THE CHILD IS GETTING HIS MESSAGE ACROSS BECAUSE, WHILE WHAT HE IS SAYING MAY NOT BE QUITE CORRECT BY ADULT STANDARDS, IT IS VERY UNDERSTANDABLE, AND THEREFORE IS GOOD COMMUNICATION.

Questions

Section 1.2 How does communication develop?

1. The baby does not communicate until he can talk. — True/False — **Marks:** 1

2. Mothers and babies communicate with each other before the baby can understand speech. Give three methods. — **Marks:** 3

3. Babies communicate with their mothers by: . . .
    Give three methods. — **Marks:** 3

4. Babies learn from the time they are born. — True/False — **Marks:** 1

5. How do babies learn about the world they live in. Give four ways. — **Marks:** 4

6. Babies use **intentional** communication when they are one week old. — True/False — **Marks:** 1

7. Jargon and first words are the same thing. — True/False — **Marks:** 1

8. Babies need to understand about turn-taking before their communication can develop. — True/False — **Marks:** 1

9. A child who uses intonation well, will be easier to understand. — True/False — **Marks:** 1

10. Generalisations are part of normal developing language. — True/False — **Marks:** 1

11. Children's language sounds the same as adult language. — True/False — **Marks:** 1

12. It is most important that young children say all the sounds of their language correctly. — True/False — **Marks:** 1

13. Children put words together in sentences in any way they please. — True/False — **Marks:** 1

13

Skills

Section 1.2   How does communication develop?

Activity 1

Spend some time (perhaps a morning or afternoon) with a mother and a baby of about 6 months. Observe their behaviour with each other, and answer these questions.

1. How does the baby communicate with the mother?
2. How does the mother communicate with the baby?
3. Do they understand each other?
    How do you know that they do or they don't?
4. Is the baby **intentionally** communicating?
    Give examples.

Activity 2

Now observe a child of about 3 years with his mother or an older person that the child knows well. Observe their behaviour and answer these questions.

1. Is the child communicating using **simple** sentences or **complex** sentences?
    Give examples.

2. Does the child understand ideas about number, size, colour?
    How do you know?
    How could you investigate this for yourself?

3. How much does the child understand?
    More than he says.
    About the same as he says.
    Less than he says.
    Give examples and reasons for your answer.

4. What communicative functions is the child using?
    List the communicative functions and give examples from the child's speech.

Activity 3

Now observe a child of about 5 years.
   Answer the questions 1,2,3 and 4 from Activity 2.

1. Compare the 3-year-old and the 5-year-old child.
    What is different about their communication skills?
    Give examples, particularly think about, **sounds**, **words**, **rules**, and **functions**.

2. Try to find out how much the 5-year-old child understands.
    Use the information you've already got in this activity and then try and find out more yourself.
    Give examples of how you would do this.

14

SECTION 1.3

How can we observe communication?

In Section 1.1 we considered 'what is communication?' and looked at different **communicative methods** and different **communicative functions**. We looked at **verbal** and **non-verbal** communication. In Skills 1.1, you watched different groups of people communicating and tried to observe them.

In Section 1.2 we considered how babies learn to communicate and develop their communication skills.

In this section we will discuss how to make these observations more specific. Speech therapists and others use special assessments to observe disordered communication, but this section suggests assessments to use **when there is no speech therapist**.

Observation of communication needs to include:

1. the communicative functions being used, and
2. the communicative methods being used.

We can ask the following **questions**:

1. Does the child communicate spontaneously or only when stimulated or asked questions by someone else?
   Observe and listen to his output.
2. How does the child communicate?
   By noises, by touching, by facial expression?
   (Which method of communication?)
3. Does the child use words? (Is he verbal?)
4. Does he say words clearly? (Is he intelligible, clear enough to understand?)
5. Does he combine words into sentences? (Does he use the rules of language?)

6. Is he understood easily by other people?
7. Does he respond at all to voices?
8. Does the child understand what is said to him?
9. Does he appear to be distracted, not listening and attending, or disinterested?

These are some of the questions we should ask and from these questions we can build up a simple observation chart to record our observations. (Sample observation charts for output and input are shown below and opposite.) Let us look at some of these observations in more detail.

We need to be sure that the child himself is able to initiate (start) communication. This is much more difficult than simply responding. Before looking at his communication in any detail we want to see if he initiates by sound, words or gesture or if he is still only at the stage of responding.

Name of child_____		Name of observer_____		
Date of observation_____		Place observed_____		
1. Observing the child's output	Yes	No	Unsure	Comments
A Child initiates communication				
B Child responds only to others communication				

C Child
  – makes noises
  – makes noises to attract attention
  – makes single sounds e.g. baba mama
  – uses single words
  – 5 words
  – 10 words
  – 20 words
  – many words				

D Child combines words
  – 2 words
  – 2/3 words
  – many words				

E Child speaks clearly				
F The child does not speak but uses his hands to gesture or point				
G He does not speak but uses his eyes and/or face to communicate				

2.	Observing the child's input	Yes	No	Unsure	Comments
A	Does the child respond – to sound? – to loud sound only? – to all sounds?				
B	Does he become bored/inattentive?				
C	Does he look towards voices?				
D	Does he like stories?				
E	Does he like being sung to?				
F	Does he understand some words?				
G	Can he fetch something for you?				
H	Can he fetch something from another room or from outside?				
I	Can he understand simple instructions e.g. 'get the cup'.				
J	Can he understand more complex instructions e.g. 'put the cup on the chair'.				

We need to know if the child makes noises. As we saw in Section 1.2, all children make noises before they use words – it is a developmental process. Our observations help us to see if the child is at an early stage in developing communication where he only makes noises or if he is beginning to try and make words.

We will see in Part 2 with our observations of a child's hearing and/or hearing loss, that response to noise is very important.

When we listen to a young child talking, we do not expect his 'words' to be as clear as an adults. A child is said to be using a word when his pattern of sound is always the same (is consistent) for a given object/action.

In a society where many languages are used, it is useful to note which language the child is using.

As we saw in Section 1.2 children do not use the rules of adult sentences from the beginning. They put words together, but do not form adult sentences. We are interested to observe if a child is using word combinations – it gives us an idea about his use of language (his output). We can see whether it is improving. We need to observe combinations of words, e.g. 'daddy go', 'daddy dinner', 'mummy cup' to see improvement from when the child was just saying strings or lists of words, e.g. 'daddy', 'dinner', 'mummy', 'cup', 'goat'. These strings or lists are just individual words and not the beginnings of sentences like the combinations of words.

We want to observe the child's **output**, his **input** and his **non-verbal communication**.

Output

- Is it clear (understood by most people)?
- Does he use names (nouns), e.g. man, cat, mummy?
- Does he use action words (verbs), e.g. go, eat, run?
- Does he use describing words (adjectives), e.g. big, hot, red?
- Does he show tense by talking about things that happened in the past (past tense) and things that are going to happen (future tense), or does he just talk about things that are happening here and now (present tense)?
- Does he indicate number?

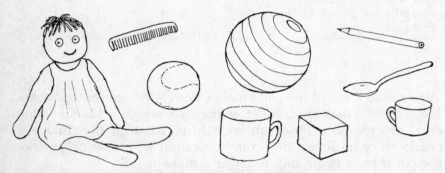

Objects that could be used to assess a child's understanding

Input

Lots of what the child understands comes from clues he gets from his surroundings and non-verbal communication from the adult who is talking to him. For example, the child is asked to 'get the spoon' when his mother is cooking or 'open the door' when his mother wants to go out of the door but has things in her hands so can't open it herself. There are lots of clues here about the communication that do not come from the verbal language the mother is using. So, the child may half understand the sentence, perhaps understanding the words 'spoon' or 'door' and guess the rest by the situation and the way the mother looks towards the door.

We can make the instructions for the child to follow, slightly

18

more complicated. For example, 'Put the cup on the chair'. As cups do not usually go on the chair, the child has to understand all the verbal language because there is no help from her past experience (what she has already learnt about where cups go). If we said, 'Put the cups on the table,' she could use her past experience, because cups usually go on the table and she would not have to understand all the verbal communication.

If the child is asked to get something from another room, this gives a clearer picture of the child's understanding as she is not being helped by extra clues like eye pointing. She also has to remember the message for longer than if she is asked to do something in the same room.

A child demonstrating understanding of verbal language without extra visual or gestural clues

Mothers are usually very sensitive to the fact that their child is not attentive or not understanding. They may not admit to a problem at first, because they hope that the child will improve. If the parent is worried about their child's communication, they are usually right in their observations. So do **listen** to the mother's worries about hearing and understanding.

Children will sometimes give the impression of understanding more than they really do.

Non-verbal communication

We want to observe the child's non-verbal (non-talking) communication too, e.g. use of gesture and facial expression. We want to know whether the child just uses non-verbal communication because he can't talk, or whether he is using non-verbal communication to help his verbal communication. If he is using it to help his talking, we want to know whether it is because:

- He can talk but is unclear and people cannot understand him.
- He can't talk because he hasn't got enough language (words) to say.

Questions

Section 1.3   How can we observe communication?

1.	It is important that children's language sounds correct.	True/False	**Marks:**	1
2.	Children who do not say words like an adult says them, have a disorder of speech.	True/False	**Marks:**	1
3.	Children use sentences from an early age.	True/False	**Marks:**	1
4.	Mothers usually recognise when there is something wrong with their child's communication.	True/False	**Marks:**	1
5.	After using single words, children use full sentences.	True/False	**Marks:**	1
6.	What is eye pointing?		**Marks:**	1
7.	Guessing is part of understanding in the young.	True/False	**Marks:**	1
8.	Children learn to talk before they understand.	True/False	**Marks:**	1
9.	We should observe output more than input.	True/False	**Marks:**	1
10.	All babies look towards voices.	True/False	**Marks:**	1
11.	List four parts of communication you could observe in the non-verbal child.		**Marks:**	4
12.	List four ways you can observe a child's understanding of communication.		**Marks:**	4
13.	Children using more than one language will be slow to develop communication.	True/False	**Marks:**	1
14.	The language of education is better than the home language.	True/False	**Marks:**	1

Skills

Section 1.3　How can we observe communication?

1. In 1.3 we discussed how we can observe children learning to use words. With a friend make a list of some of the words which young children commonly learn early.
    a. List 10/20 object words (nouns) which children often learn first. (Words for food, family members and animals are often learned early.)
    b. List 10 action words (verbs) which children often learn early.
    c. List 10 describing words (adjectives) which children often learn early.

2. Which language does the child use at home? at market? Make two lists of words if these are different.
    What sort of gestures have you observed being used by young children?
    With a friend discuss whether these gestures/pointing/facial expression in a young child become less acceptable among older handicapped children.

3. List examples of different **communicative functions** e.g.:
    a. Responding to something.
    b. Asking/requesting.
    c. Agreeing.
    d. Disagreeing.
    e. Expanding on something (perhaps by describing).
    Give examples of these functions as used by a child:
    *   around 2 years
    *   around 3 years
    *   around 5 years

4. Are these examples
    *   of spoken communicative functions?
    *   of non-verbal communicative functions?
    *   of mixed spoken and non-verbal?

5. With a friend make a list of simple instructions which you ask a child to undertake (as in examples on pages 18 and 19).
    Can you ensure that these simple instructions do not rely on visual clues?

6. We know and you have observed that young children do not use words as clearly as adults.
    a. With a friend make a list of the sounds of your language with which young children have difficulty.
    b. Do young children have difficulty in making some sounds at the beginning, the end or the middle of words? Discuss this carefully with your friend.

SECTION 1.4

How can the development of communication go wrong?

We learnt in Sections 1.1 and 1.2 about communication and how it develops. This section is going to mention briefly some of the areas where communication development can go wrong or break down. It should help you to recognise what is wrong with a child's speech and direct you to other sections of the book where you can find out more.

Interaction skills

Building interaction skills with the mother or caregiver can sometimes go wrong. The child is particularly at risk if he is handicapped in some way.

1. If he is deaf, he will not hear what is being said, and may not respond.
2. If he is blind, he cannot see his parent and will miss all the visual signs that are so important during the building of a close relationship for interaction.
3. If he is physically handicapped, he may take so long to co-ordinate his muscles to respond appropriately that his response is missed by his parent who has gone on to do other things.
4. If he is mentally handicapped, he may take a long time to understand what is being said and like the physically handicapped child his response may be so late that it is missed.

We will find out more about interaction in disabled children in Parts 3 and 4.

If he has more than one handicap, he is even more at risk.

Initiation

Building interaction skills also involves the child learning to initiate (start) communication and control the interaction. This can go wrong for the same reasons that are listed above.

You will find out more about initiation and how to encourage it in Part 3.

Before he begins to talk, the child may not have built:

1. a good non-verbal framework where he intentionally communicates;
2. turn-taking skills where he can take control of the conversation.

This non-verbal framework consists of pre-verbal skills. Part 3 has more information about pre-verbal skills and lots of ideas for encouraging their development especially in mentally handicapped children.

Listening and attending

Sometimes there are problems with listening and attending to speech sounds and words, or just generally to what is going on around the child. This means that the child often does not hear all of what is said to him. He therefore may not reply appropriately and communication may break down.

When communication breaks down, the adult needs to know how to help the child to **repair** the communication. The adult needs to know how to encourage the child to try and send his message again, perhaps in a different way. The way the adult talks to the child will make a difference to the way the child replies to the adult. You will find out more about this in Parts 2 and 3.

Sounds

Sometimes the child has difficulty saying the sounds of the language correctly. This makes his speech difficult to understand for people listening. This may be because:

1. He doesn't hear them correctly.
2. He is rather slow at learning them.
3. He has something wrong with his speech muscles and or the nerves that make them work.

Try and decide why the child's speech is difficult to understand – hearing, slow learning or physical movements. It might be a

This child is finding it difficult to make her unclear speech understood by her friends

combination of these reasons. You will find information on hearing in Part 2, information on slow learners and encouraging language development generally in Part 3 and information on physical problems in Part 4.

Words

Sometimes the child has difficulty with words and putting what he wants to say into words. This might be because he has learning difficulties.

Information on encouraging language development can be found in Part 3.

Language rules

Sometimes the child has difficulty linking words together in the right order, i.e. by rules. This might be because he has learning difficulties or a specific problem with learning language.

Look in Part 3 for information about encouraging language development.

Melody

Sometimes, particularly if the child has hearing difficulties he might not have much melody in his language. It sounds all on one note (on a monotone). Lots of information about the meaning of what you are saying is carried in the melody of your speech (your intonation) both for the listener and the speaker.

Part 2 is all about hearing and the child with a hearing loss. Look there for more information about deafness, what to do about it, and helping the deaf child to communicate.

Questions

Section 1.4   How can the development of communication go wrong?

1.	Interaction skills are not important.	True/False	**Marks:**	1
2.	Children can communicate well if they just respond to what is said to them.	True/False	**Marks:**	1
3.	Being able to see is not essential for learning to communicate.	True/False	**Marks:**	1
4.	Physical handicap does not affect communication skills.	True/False	**Marks:**	1
5.	Mental handicap does not affect communication skills.	True/False	**Marks:**	1
6.	Children who can hear do not have problems with listening.	True/False	**Marks:**	1
7.	Some handicaps affect the development of communication. Name four of them.		**Marks:**	4
8.	Not being able to say sounds properly is one way that speech can go wrong. Name four reasons for this.		**Marks:**	4
9.	Talking all the time is good communication.	True/False	**Marks:**	1
10.	When a child is silent it means he cannot communicate.	True/False	**Marks:**	1
11.	Deaf children cannot communicate.	True/False	**Marks:**	1
12.	Good communicators: a. talk a lot, b. listen a lot, c. talk and listen Select a, b, or c.	True/False	**Marks:**	1
13.	A child who misses out words cannot communicate.	True/False	**Marks:**	1
14.	You can only communicate through talking.	True/False	**Marks:**	1

Skills

Section 1.4 How can the development of communication go wrong?

Activity 1

1. Observe a normal baby of 6 months to 1 year and his mother.
2. How do they show that they have learnt about turn-taking?
3. Who controls the interaction?
4. How do you know this?

Activity 2

Now repeat Activity 1 with a handicapped baby, writing down the answers to questions 1–4.
Write down how the child is handicapped.
Then answer these questions:

1. How is the relationship between the mother and baby different?

2. What suggestions could you make to help the mother create a more natural relationship.

Activity 3

Observe a child who can talk, but is having communication difficulties.

1. Are the child's communication difficulties in:
   a. understanding,
   b. expressing,
   c. both.
Give reasons for your answer.

2. If the child is having difficulties expressing, which bits of her expression are causing problems? Is it:
   a. sounds,
   b. meaning (words),
   c. rules (linking the words together),
   d. melody (the musical ups and downs of speech).
Give examples from the communication you have observed.

3. What suggestions could you make that might help her to communicate more effectively.

PART 2

Hearing and Hearing Loss

SECTION 2.1

What is sound, what is hearing, how do we hear?

Before we can begin to consider hearing loss or deafness as it is often called we must consider three questions.

1. What is sound?
2. What is hearing?
3. How do we hear?

What is sound?

We can consider two aspects of sound: **frequency** (or the pitch of a sound) and **intensity** (or the loudness of a sound).

Frequency (pitch)

Speech and most of the sounds around us do not consist of pure tones (like a musical note) of a given pitch, rather speech and other sounds round about us (environmental sounds) consist of complex patterns of tones. We divide these patterns of tones broadly into:

1. Low frequency sounds, e.g. a wooden spoon banging on a table or the speech sound 'ooo' or 'mm'.
2. Middle frequency sounds, e.g. a wooden spoon banging a large metal pot or the speech sound 'd' or 'b'.
3. High frequency sounds, e.g. metal spoon gently banging a thin small metal pan or the rustle of a sweet wrapper or the speech sound 'sss' or 'shsh'.

Intensity (loudness)

Loudness is a result of how intense a sound is at the point it is made. We, with normal hearing all understand what loudness is but probably could not measure it. Loudness is measured in decibels (db). We need not be concerned with what a decibel is but need to understand the approximate decibel levels of some simple environmental sounds around us. By understanding how loud these environmental sounds are we can begin to understand what sounds a deaf child with a particular hearing loss will be unable to hear.

For someone with normal hearing these are approximate measurements of loudness:

- 30 db would be a whispered voice 2 metres away
- 50 db conversation voice 2 metres away
- 70 db a very loud voice 2 metres away
- 90 db a nearby lorry going up a hill changing gear
- 110 db an aeroplane taking off very nearby or a loudspeaker at a very noisy disco
- 120 db the threshold of pain

What is hearing and how do we hear?

The simple answer to that question is that we hear primarily with our ears. To understand this more fully we must consider what happens in the ear. There are three parts to the ear:

1. The **outer ear**, the part we can see.
2. The **middle ear**, inside the person's head, we cannot see it.
3. The **inner ear**, again inside the person's head, and not seen.

This text will not give great detail about the ear, almost any book concerned with human biology will have a fuller account of the anatomy of the ear and if readers wish further information (or have studied this as part of their school certificate biology course) they should refer elsewhere.

The **outer ear** consists of the 'pinna' the part we see and the 'ear canal', that tube which we feel passing into our head. In adults the 'ear canal' is between 2.5 and 3 cm long, and in children it grows from a length of about 1.5 cm to adult size, in other words the 'ear canal' is quite short. The **outer ear** meets the **middle ear** at the ear drum.

This **ear drum** prevents anything from entering the **middle ear**.

The **middle ear** is a very small space containing three little bones. There is a small channel which passes from the middle ear to the

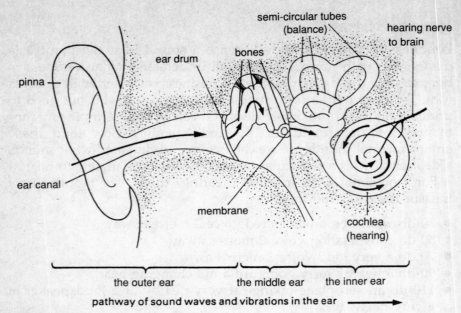

semi-circular tubes
(balance)

hearing nerve
to brain

ear drum

bones

pinna

ear canal

membrane

cochlea
(hearing)

the outer ear   the middle ear   the inner ear

pathway of sound waves and vibrations in the ear ⟶

Diagram of the ear

back of the throat. At the opposite side of the middle ear from the ear drum is another membrane which leads to the **inner ear**.

The **inner ear** has two main features: a fluid-filled structure which is concerned with hearing and another structure which is concerned with balance.

How do we hear?

In other words, how does the ear work?

The **outer ear** collects sound waves and channels them through the ear canal causing vibrations of the ear drum. These vibrations are relayed into the **middle ear**.

When the vibrations of the ear drum are relayed to the **middle ear**, they cause movements of the little bones in the middle ear and these movements in turn cause movement of the membrane which leads to the **inner ear**.

The vibrations of the membrane leading to the **inner ear** lead to vibrations of tiny hair cells in the hearing structure of the inner ear. Some of these tiny hair cells respond to high frequency sounds and others to low frequency sounds. Whichever hair cells are responding they all transmit messages through the **hearing nerve** to the brain.

In the brain the messages are recognised either as environmental sound which the person has heard before or (**if** the person has learned language) as language.

What is hearing loss?

Something may go wrong with the **outer ear** – the canal may become blocked. Either because the child has pushed something into his ear or because an infection of the **middle ear** has caused a build-up of pus which has drained into the outer ear.

Sometimes the **ear drum** may be damaged especially if it has been burst by a build-up of infected fluid in the middle ear. If the ear drum is burst, or if it heals badly after a burst, it will not vibrate well and not relay these vibrations to the middle ear as well as it should. This will lead to the child not receiving all the sound in his ear, a **partial deafness**.

The **middle ear** may not function well, either because there is an infection, or because the little bones are damaged. An infection may cause the pus to fill the middle ear. This can become very thick, in which case the little bones cannot move easily and the sound waves cannot be transmitted very well. Some ear infections cause the child a lot of pain, he cries, the ear looks red and the mother knows there is a problem with his ears and seeks help to control the infection. Other infections however do not cause pain the child does not complain a lot and the mother may not notice the problem. While the child has an ear infection (both those which hurt and those which don't) his middle ear will not be transmitting sound waves well and he will not hear well. Also if the child has repeated ear infections there may be some permanent damage to the middle ear. Deafness caused by difficulties in the middle ear is known as **conductive deafness** it may be:

- permanent or temporary,
- cause a marked deafness or a slight deafness depending on the degree of the problem.

Most ear infections can be treated by a medical practitioner and by treatment of the infection it is often possible to avoid permanent deafness.

The inner ear may not function well, either because of damage to the tiny hair cells in the hearing structure of the inner ear or because of damage to the hearing nerve which transmits messages to the brain. Deafness caused by damage to the inner ear is known as nerve deafness (or sensori neural deafness) is nearly always permanent and seldom caused by infection.

Questions

Section 2.1   What is sound, what is hearing, how do we hear?

1. Sound is made up of:
    a. different pitches (frequencies)
    b. different degrees of loudness (intensities)
    c. different pitches (frequencies) and
    loudness (intensities)
    Select a, b or c.   **Marks:**   1

2. What is the unit of measurement of   **Marks:**   1
    loudness?

3. Name three parts of the ear.   **Marks:**   3

4. Which two parts of the ear can we **not**   **Marks:**   2
    see?

5. Where is the ear drum?   **Marks:**   1

6. How does the middle ear work?   **Marks:**   1

7. What happens in the inner ear?   **Marks:**   1

8. Where do messages from the inner ear   **Marks:**   1
    pass to?

9. Why does the middle ear sometimes not   **Marks:**   1
    work well?

10. All infections of the middle ear are painful. True/False   **Marks:**   1

11. Middle ear infections are common in   True/False   **Marks:**   1
    young children.

12. Conductive deafness is caused by a
    problem
    a. of the middle ear
    b. of the inner ear.
    Select a or b.   **Marks:**   1

13. Conductive deafness is always   True/False   **Marks:**   1
    permanent

14. Sensori neural (nerve) deafness is
    caused by
    a. a problem of the outer ear
    b. a problem of the inner ear
    c. a problem of the middle ear.
    Select a, b or c.   **Marks:**   1

15. Ear infections always lead to deafness.   True/False   **Marks:**   1

16. Ear infections can be treated by a doctor.   True/False   **Marks:**   1

17. Sensori neural (nerve) deafness can   True/False   **Marks:**   1
    always be treated by a doctor.

32

SECTION 2.2

How can we observe hearing and hearing loss?

We need to observe both how a child's **hearing functions** but also how the child **uses his hearing**. It is no use at all doing only one of these, we need to do both.

Hearing functions

Here we are looking at the way the child's hearing mechanism works. The child's hearing mechanism refers to:

1. his **outer ear** – the bit you can see,
2. his **middle ear** – the bit you cannot see consisting of a chamber with three tiny bones,
3. the **inner ear** – another bit which you cannot see where the message from the ear is passed to the nerve which leads to the brain.

A child may not hear because there is something wrong with his ears. This may be because of **disease**. We need to ask the mother if her child has had an illness which she knows has affected the child's hearing.

- Has he had ear infections?
- Pussy or discharging ears?
- Many throat infections?
- Many coughs and colds?
- Does the child scratch his ears?

If the child has had a known disease of the ears the first thing to do is ask the health worker or doctor to look at the child's ears.

33

Sometimes after an illness the ears may no longer hurt but still be fluid filled and function badly.

Some children may have disease of the ear which the mother does **not know** about. If the child has had a disease that causes no pain to the ear, the mother may not have noticed. In such a case the mother may, if you ask her carefully, remember that he sometimes appears 'naughty' or 'inattentive'. What the mother may be recalling is periods when the child could not hear her very well. The health worker may see some signs of 'non-hurting' deafness.

Disease of the ear usually affects the middle ear by filling it with pus so that it cannot function well. We can tell if a child has this problem by:

1. asking the mother her opinion (most mothers seem to know if their child is not hearing well);
2. observing if the child hears better at some times than others; and
3. noticing if he scratches his ears.

Some deafness is caused during pregnancy or by birth trauma. In such cases it is usually the **inner ear** which is affected. In such a case the mother will not be able to tell you about a disease which the child has had. She may think that the child's deafness is the result of something she did or ate during pregnancy. This is **very unlikely** and she should be reassured that the child's deafness is **not her fault**. If she remains with a guilty feeling it will be very difficult for her to help the child to overcome his difficulties.

Use of hearing

The paragraphs above explain something about a child's **hearing functions** and reasons why they may not work well. We will now consider the child's **use of hearing**.

A child needs to experience sound before he can use his hearing well. If he is very isolated and not spoken to, cuddled, and loved he may become very withdrawn and not respond to sound like other children. For such a child sound, especially talking, has no meaning for him.

The first way we can observe a child's hearing then is to **ask the mother or other family members some questions**, e.g.

1. Has he had ear infections or sore ears?
2. Does he scratch his ears?
3. Are there times when his hearing seems worse than others?

4. Does he attend to sound? what sort of sound?
5. Does he attend to talking/singing?

The next stage is to observe the child yourself. How does he respond to sounds in the home? e.g. does he turn if a dog barks?, if someone calls?, if he hears the door bang?, if he hears a biscuit or sweet packet being opened? These observations will tell you if he **responds to environmental sounds**. You must then observe if this response is only to very loud and very nearby sounds or if he is also responding to quite quiet and distant sounds.

You can then confirm your observations with a simple test using soundmakers. (See Skills 2.2 Activity 3.) What we are trying to do is to see if the child has a hearing loss which is:

- **mild or moderate or severe,**
- **there all the time or only sometimes,**
- **a middle ear deafness which can be cured, or**
- **a permanent deafness which usually cannot be cured.**

You can also watch how the child tries to communicate with other people. Does he make noises? Do these sound like the noises most children make? Or do they sound different? Does he speak clearly? Is he learning to speak at the same age as other children or is he slower? Does he point to things or use a lot of gestures? Answers to questions will tell you the **effect of deafness on his developing communication**.

Observe the child's behaviour, does he respond like a child of his age or like a younger child? Is he friendly or withdrawn? Does he play with other children? Does he help in the house or garden? Answers to these questions will tell you something about **his social development**.

It is also important to find out what the mother feels. Does she try to hide the problem? This **denial** in parents is not helpful in rehabilitation. Does she say that the child is stupid or naughty? This may be because nobody has explained how she can help the child, but this **anger** is an attitude which is very damaging for the child's development. Does she feel that it is her fault that the child is deaf? **Guilt** on the part of the mother is also not helpful.

Questions

Section 2.2 How can we observe hearing and hearing loss?

1. You need specialist equipment to tell if a child is very deaf. — True/False — **Marks:** 1

2. Deafness is always caused by disease. — True/False — **Marks:** 1

3. Once a child is deaf there is nothing that can be done for him. — True/False — **Marks:** 1

4. Deaf children always have deaf parents. — True/False — **Marks:** 1

5. Deaf children cannot communicate. They are dumb. — True/False — **Marks:** 1

6. A child who is deaf is also stupid. — True/False — **Marks:** 1

7. All deaf children have the same degree of deafness. — True/False — **Marks:** 1

8. Why might mothers' answers to questions about their child's hearing not always be accurate? — **Marks:** 1

9. List three degrees of deafness. — **Marks:** 3

10. Deaf children are always naughty. — True/False — **Marks:** 1

11. Which deaf children would you always refer to a doctor? — **Marks:** 1

12. Describe three symptoms which may lead you to suspect that a child has a middle ear infection. — **Marks:** 3

13. Things that the mother eats in pregnancy cause deafness. — True/False — **Marks:** 1

14. List three ways in which a deaf child's social development may be different. — **Marks:** 3

Skills

Section 2.2 How can we observe hearing and hearing loss?

Activity 1

Make a list of noises which occur in the house; these are known as **environmental noises**, e.g.

- stirring a spoon in a pot,
- pouring water,
- banging a door,
- a dog barking,
- a telephone ringing,
- a radio being switched on.

Make the list as long as you can, about 30 noises.

Look at this list. Which of the noises can you control by switching them on/off or by start/stopping? Keep on your list those which you can control and strike out those which you can not control.

Look at the list again and divide it into three groups:

- loud noises
- quiet noises
- middling noises.

Try to make sure you have 10 noises in each group. Check your list of environmental noises with a friend. You can use this list to help you observe a child's response to environmental noises. Does the child turn round (or respond in other ways) to loud noises? To quiet noises? To middling noises?

Activity 2

Mothers are often aware that their child has difficulty with hearing.

1. Make a list of questions which you might ask a mother about her child. Write a full list of questions.

2. Try to divide these questions into two groups, those questions which are **closed questions** (they need the answer yes or no) e.g.:
   - Does your child scratch his ears?
   - Do his ears discharge?
   - Does he talk like other children?

   and secondly a list of **open questions** (which allow the mother to describe things) e.g.:
   - How does he respond to a loud noise?
   - What does he do if you call his name?

   Usually questions which start 'does' are closed questions and questions which start 'how' are open questions.

Activity 3

What would you do if a mother denies the problem? Make a plan of how you can bring her to accept that her child has a hearing problem.

Devise a checklist of ten simple questions which a village worker could ask a mother in order to establish if the mothers child has a hearing loss. Try to ask questions which are:

- open rather than closed,
- not 'loaded' with an answer which could be thought to be the 'right' answer,
- enable the mother to describe the child (3–5-year-old child).

Activity 4

You do not need a lot of specialist equipment to tell if a child is deaf. You can find out some of the problems with very simple sound makers.

Take three tins:

- put about 10 grains of rice in tin No 1,
- put about 10 large beans into tin No 2,
- put a piece of wood into tin No 3.

Label the tins and cover the holes. If you shake the tins gently you will find that they make sounds with higher (tin 1), middle (tin 2) and low (tin 3) frequencies. If you shake more strongly each will sound louder.

Try shaking the tins near the child while someone else distracts him (makes him look forwards, away from you). Make sure the child does not **see** you. How does he respond to the noises?

If you suspect a hearing loss try to have him properly assessed at a centre where they may be able to help more.

SECTION 2.3

Helping a deaf child to develop communication

Giving the deaf child a chance

Deaf children are not 'dumb'. Deaf children will without any help develop some form of communication although they may not sound or look like us when they communicate. With help most deaf children can develop good communication skills that are understood by others.

If we continue to think of deaf children as 'dumb' we suggest that there is nothing that can be done to help that child and his family to improve his communication. This is not true. We can help.

Helping the deaf child's communication

We saw in Sections 1.1 and 1.2 that young children communicate using a lot of different **communicative methods** and that although they gradually learn to use spoken language as their main method of communication they do still keep the use of other (often non-verbal) methods.

We saw also in Sections 1.1 and 1.2 that young children used different **communicative functions** as they were developing their language and communication skills. They learn to ask, to tell, to agree, to greet etc.

Thirdly we saw in Section 1.2 that turn-taking is a very important part of early language development.

When we consider deaf children's language development these three points are just as important.

1. The deaf child must be talked to, read to, sung to, played with just like families do with hearing children, so that the deaf child learns about turn-taking and learns to enjoy communication. Often when the family learn that the child is deaf they stop doing these things. This is wrong. The deaf child needs this input just as much, and in some ways more than a hearing child.
2. The deaf child must be given the opportunity to communicate. He needs to practice using different **communicative functions** just like the hearing child and will not get this chance if his needs are always supplied without him needing to communicate. For example, wait until he asks for a drink (either by pointing or by gesturing or by some sound), give him some choices so that he learns to indicate yes and no.
3. The deaf child is unlikely to use spoken language as his main **communicative method** but he will use other methods, pointing, gestures, noises, the family must encourage the use of these different methods. If they accept only speech and put a lot of pressure on the child to say words he may become very frustrated. Sometimes this frustration shows itself as naughty behaviour or as withdrawal by the child. It will not help the deaf child to communicate better or to stop being naughty if he is beaten. It is more likely to make him worse.

The family will need help to understand these ideas.

1. They must communicate and talk to the deaf child as much as they can. They may feel that the deaf child is not improving and that talking to him is not helping. The CBR worker will need to help the family to understand that any development of the deaf child's communication or his understanding of turn-taking is going to be slow and that they should not give up.
2. They may feel that in a busy family it is easier to just do things for the deaf child or give him things rather than wait for him to ask or to tell them things. It is true it may be quicker for the family but they will need help to understand that the child must be given the chance to use different communicative functions.
3. The family may not like the deaf child to use different communicative methods like pointing or gestures or making noises because strangers notice this unusual behaviour of the child and make remarks. The family may find that embarrassing and prefer the deaf child to remain silent. That may help the family's embarrassment but it will not help the deaf child at all. The CBR worker can help the family to see that it is better to think of the child's needs rather than their own embarrassment.

Helping the deaf child to develop language

We saw above how important it is to help the deaf child to:

- develop communication skills,
- use these communication skills,
- be encouraged by his family, and
- not feel that his family are embarrassed by his attempts.

If the deaf child begins to communicate easily in the family and gain in confidence then, **but only then**, may be the time to help his development of spoken language. It is no use trying to help a deaf child to speak if he is not able to communicate. He is a child not a parrot!

The ease with which a deaf child begins to learn spoken language will depend on several things:

1. How deaf the child is – children who are less deaf will learn to speak more easily than children who are very deaf.
2. When he became deaf – if he has had several months or years of hearing before he went deaf his speech will be clearer.
3. Whether he has a hearing aid – deaf children with a good hearing aid and an earmould which has been made for them will usually learn to talk more easily than a child with a similar deafness but no hearing aid (see Section 2.5 for some information about hearing aids).
4. Whether he has other handicaps – a deaf child with cerebral palsy or a deaf child with mental handicap will have much greater difficulties in learning to speak.

The family will need help to understand these things. They need to know that learning to talk is very difficult for all deaf children and very very difficult for some. The family will need to understand this if they are to encourage the child's attempts with great patience.

What to do

The deaf child should be spoken to clearly **but not** with funny lip movements or by shouting. The family should try to use the same words for things, e.g. it will be very confusing if father asks the child to 'get the bucket' and mother asks him to 'get the pail'.

The family, with the help of the CBR worker should work out a short list of words which would be **useful** to the child and use these words regularly and clearly. Remember the important thing is to **use** the words not just repeat them. The words should be

Let's sit on the mat and play with the ball.

An adult talking to a deaf child using clear speech

useful words (there is little point in the word 'elephant' if the child never sees one!). **Input** goes before **output** (the child must hear/see the words often before he will use them).

Words which show clear patterns on the lips may be easier for the child e.g. 'bed' is easier to see on the lips than 'chair', 'sheep' is easier to see on the lips than 'goat'. The lip patterns of words may be something you need to consider when you make a list of useful words for the child to learn with the family.

His speech sounds funny

Yes it will. Most deaf people (except perhaps those who became deaf after the age of 10 years) will sound different. The family must be helped not to be embarrassed by this. The important thing is for the child to begin to understand some words and then to use them. The family will usually understand his words even if they sound different. If the CBR worker or family tries to make the child think too much about the sounds of his words he may become frustrated, angry or give up trying.

The CBR worker and perhaps the deaf child's brothers and sisters can try to explain to the other children why he sounds different and try to prevent too much teasing.

Questions

Section 2.3   Helping a deaf child to develop communication

1. Deaf children are usually deaf and dumb. True/False **Marks:** 1

2. List three communicative methods used **Marks:** 3
    by a deaf child.

3. List three communicative functions used **Marks:** 3
    by a deaf child.

4. Deaf children have difficulty with:
    a. understanding and using spoken
    language,
    b. using spoken language,
    c. understanding spoken language.
    Select a, b or c. **Marks:** 1

5. A deaf child's social development is the True/False **Marks:** 1
    same as that of a hearing child.

6. Deaf children cannot ask for things. True/False **Marks:** 1

7. Slightly deaf children learn to speak more True/False **Marks:** 1
    easily than very deaf children.

8. Children who become deaf later in True/False **Marks:** 1
    childhood (acquired deafness) cannot
    speak at all.

9. Hearing aids if properly matched to a deaf True/False **Marks:** 1
    child's needs are very helpful.

10. Give two examples of useful words which **Marks:** 2
    are easy to see on the lips.

11. Deaf children cannot learn to talk. True/False **Marks:** 1

12. Deaf children are stupid because they do True/False **Marks:** 1
    not talk.

13. Families of deaf children should speak to True/False **Marks:** 1
    them clearly and often.

14. You need to shout to deaf children. True/False **Marks:** 1

15. Deaf children do not mind being teased. True/False **Marks:** 1

Skills

Section 2.3   How can we help the deaf child to develop language?

Activity 1

Make a list of communicative functions which you could encourage a mother to use with her deaf 3-year-old child. For example:

1. Asking for a drink rather than just being given one, the mother could quietly hold the child's cup just out of reach and say (looking at the child) 'cup' or 'water' and give it to the child when he points or makes a noise.

2. Indicating choice, the mother can give him a choice, holding an orange in one hand and a banana in the other (both slightly out of reach and looking at the child's face) she can say 'orange' or 'banana' if the child points to one or makes a choice, he can be given the fruit he has chosen.

3. By indicating yes and no, if there is a food, a tee shirt, a toy which the child does not like the mother can offer it to him and if he indicates 'no' clearly she should accept his communication and take it away.

   Think of some others, try to make them real functions rather than very artificial ones, things the family would do anyway. Discuss your list with a friend.

Activity 2

Try to let the family see how difficult it is to communicate without speech. Ask them to have a whole mealtime when no one is allowed to **say** anything. The family will soon see how difficult it is to let their needs be known but they will also see how pointing and gestures can help. This exercise should help the hearing people in the family to:

1. see how difficult it is for the deaf person,

2. understand how important gesture and pointing are if you cannot speak.

If you are in a culture where pointing is rather rude, consider the effects of this on a young deaf child. Could you make it possible for a deaf child to point e.g. in the home?

Activity 3

Practice 'speaking clearly' this does not mean shouting, it means:

1. looking at the other (deaf) person in the face as you speak;

2. making clear lip movements (but not too much so);

3. using facial expression;

4. using some gestures (but not too much);

5. using simple words and short sentences;

6. changing the word to a similar one if the person does not understand you.

Do you feel you could teach someone to 'speak clearly'?

If you come from a culture where looking at the other person in the face is considered rather rude consider the effects on a deaf child. Could he look at the faces of family members and could they look directly at him?

Activity 4

Make a list of useful words which are 'easy to see on the lips'. Make sure these are useful words to the child. Usually short or two syllable words starting with 'p', 'b', 'm', 'w', 'f', 'v', 'th' and followed by a vowel will be easier to see. Check this list with a friend.

Activity 5

Try to meet a deaf adult who is able to work. This person will help you to understand a bit more about the problems of deafness but if he is able to hold a job he will also show how deaf people can succeed. This deaf person may be willing to talk to the family. Most deaf children have hearing parents and some deaf children are born to families who have no deaf family members at all. In these cases the family feel frightened of the deafness and the mother may feel guilty. It may help if you, the CBR worker, can get to know one or two deaf people who may be prepared to see the family of a deaf child. Even if they cannot talk to each other very well it may help the family to meet a deaf adult.

Activity 6

Find out if there is a national organisation for deaf people, or one for parents of deaf children. Such organisations often have leaflets which they will send you and which may be useful. They may also have leaflets for you to give to the parents. Remember most parents cannot cope with too much information. The CBR worker will need to help them with leaflets. The nearest school for the deaf may have some leaflets or other information, even for children who are not able to go to their school.

SECTION 2.4

Can we help a deaf child to attend school?

Schools for the deaf

Most countries of the world have some specialist schools for the deaf. Deaf children may be sent to these schools where they should be given:

- a hearing aid for their needs, and
- specialist teaching.

The disadvantage of some schools for the deaf for **some families** is that they are:

- a long way from the child's home,
- can be expensive,
- may teach the child in a language which is not spoken in his village or his family.

The disadvantages of distance and use of a different language in the school can further isolate a deaf child from his family and neighbours when he comes home for the long holidays. When he does come home for holidays, he is no longer one of the group of friends in the village, he feels separated from his parents, brothers and sisters and he may now speak the language which is taught in school rather than his home language.

The choice of whether to send their child to a school for the deaf (if there is one) will be made by the family. The CBR worker can help by helping the family to understand the advantages and disadvantages **and** any alternatives which may be available.

The rest of this Section is written as if the deaf child cannot go to a school for the deaf and will remain in the village or community.

Can the deaf child go to the village school?

The answer to this is maybe. The answer is going to depend on a lot of factors for example:

1. How deaf the child is – it is going to be easier to integrate a slightly deaf child into the village school than a very deaf child.
2. Has he been deaf from birth or from an accident/illness in later childhood (acquired deafness) – it is probably going to be easier to integrate an acquired deaf child into the school.
3. Whether the deaf child has other handicaps – it is going to be easier if there are no other handicaps.
4. Whether the child has a hearing aid and whether his family really understand how to use and care for it – if the child has a good aid and has been taught how to use it it will be easier to integrate him into the village school.
5. The attitude of the village teacher – this is in some ways the **most important factor**. If the teacher does not really want the deaf child in his school he will make it difficult for the deaf child but if he is really willing to try to integrate the child there is a chance of success.

The deaf child's communication skills at school entry

Hearing children can understand a lot of what is said to them and can speak quite clearly before they go to school. The communication skills and developing language skills of a deaf child are also an important consideration before deciding if a deaf child could cope with the village school. To even consider the village school as a possibility the deaf child must have developed:

1. good communication skills to let his wants be known,
2. some understanding of spoken language, and
3. use of some spoken words.

Let us consider these three points in a little detail.

1. If the deaf child cannot let his needs be known e.g. when he wants to go to the lavatory, when he does not feel well, he is likely to behave differently from the other children, be teased, perhaps be disruptive in the classroom etc.

46

2. If the deaf child has very poor <u>understanding skills</u>, he will not be able to begin to learn in a big classroom and he will probably become disruptive. If he cannot understand, his behaviour in class is likely to get worse as he becomes more frustrated.
3. If the deaf child uses some spoken words properly (even if they are not completely clear) he may then be ready to start learning written words also.

Written language

Most hearing children learn to speak before they learn to write. For some intelligent deaf children, learning to read and write words can help their spoken language (both their use of spoken language and their understanding). If the deaf child has a slight hearing loss, no other handicaps and is understanding and using some words before he goes to school he may be able to cope with the school, learn and develop but only with the co-operation of the village teacher.

How can the CBR worker help the village teacher to help the deaf child?

If the village teacher is willing to take the deaf child into school there are certain things the CBR worker can do to make it easier for teacher and child:

1. Help the teacher to understand a little about deafness.
2. Try to help the teacher to understand how deaf the child is, give examples of the sorts of things he **can** hear and the things he **cannot** hear (Section 2.1 page 29).
3. Explain how difficult communication is for deaf children and describe the deaf child's communication skills, **be honest, do not pretend to the teacher that the child is better than he is**.
4. If the child has a hearing aid explain it to the teacher (see Section 2.5 below).
5. Talk about the best place for the deaf child to sit, near the front and near the window.
6. Explain about 'speaking clearly' (Section 2.3).
7. Explain that the deaf child will find school quite tiring and may find half days enough (this may be enough for the teacher too!).

This is a lot of new information for the village teacher who is already very busy and the CBR worker is going to have to be very tactful to persuade him that this is not too much new work.

Sign language

Let us consider very deaf children. If we think back to Section 2.1 when we considered sound, we mean those children who cannot hear very loud noises, e.g. a lorry changing gear as it goes up a hill beside you. These very deaf children will have great difficulty in learning to understand spoken language and in learning to speak. Such children will naturally prefer to use gestures and will probably be better using sign language. Sign language is taught in many schools for the deaf to the very deaf pupils and we know now that very deaf children find it easier to learn written and spoken language if they have developed sign language first. It used to be thought that sign language interfered with the learning of spoken languages, this is not strictly true for very deaf children.

How can a child who is not going to a school for the deaf learn sign language? This is difficult but there are two things the CBR worker can do:

1. Encourage the child and his family to use natural gestures to both help him to understand things and express things, **and to remain patient and not to beat the child**.
2. See if there is a deaf family member or other deaf person in the village or community who would be able and willing to teach the deaf child and his family some signs. If the child and his family learn the signs that are used by deaf people in his country, when he is older he will be more widely understood by other deaf people than if he uses the 'home made' natural gestures of his family.

If there is such a deaf person who could help to teach the deaf child some signs the CBR worker will have to try to check that this goes well. The adult deaf person will probably never have been asked to be a teacher before and will need to understand what is wanted of him and the CBR worker will have to check that the child is learning. Perhaps the deaf person could visit the deaf child's home one or two times each week.

Summary of what the CBR worker can do

1. Discuss the advantages and disadvantages of school for the deaf with the family.

    *   advantages
        - special teaching
        - hearing aids

48

- disadvantages
  - distance
  - cost
  - which language?

2. Consider whether the deaf child **could** cope with the local school. This check-list includes some of the factors that the CBR worker will have to consider and discuss with the parents and village teacher:
   - degree of deafness;
   - whether it is an acquired deafness;
   - whether the child has other handicaps;
   - whether the child has a hearing aid and uses it well;
   - the attitude of the teacher; and
   - the child's communication skills.

3. Discuss with the teacher the possibility of having the deaf child in his school. The following list includes some of the points to discuss:
   - what deafness is;
   - how deaf this particular child is;
   - what communication difficulties this child has;
   - how his hearing aid works (if he has one);
   - the best place for the child to sit; and
   - 'clear speaking'.

4. With a very deaf child the CBR worker may have to think not about how to get the child into the village school because this may be unrealistic but rather how to try to give him some sign language training.

SECTION 2.5

What about hearing aids?

A CBR worker will never be in a position to give a hearing aid to a deaf child. This is a specialised and difficult task that will be done by trained staff usually at a centre or perhaps at an outreach 'hearing camp' or similar.

However, hearing aids are so important to deaf children that we feel it is important that CBR workers understand something about hearing aids so that they can make sure that the child is using it well, if there is nobody else doing this.

How can you learn about hearing aids?

If there is a child in your village/community with a hearing aid he must have got it from somewhere. Perhaps the easiest way to find out about hearing aids is to make an appointment and visit that centre (if it is not too far away). They can tell you some of the advice they give to children and their families about the use of hearing aids and about simple maintenance.

If such a visit is not possible the following paragraphs will give you some information.

What is a hearing aid?

It is a piece of equipment which makes sound louder. There are several main pieces to all hearing aids:

1/2. A receiver/microphone which picks up sounds and changes sound to electrical impulses (a sort of electrical message).
3. An amplifier which makes the impulses bigger (increases the size of the electrical message).
4. A battery which makes the microphone and amplifier work.

5. An ear piece (ear mould) which leads the increased sound into the outer ear to the ear drum.
6. A cable or piece of tube which connects 1/2 and 3 to 4.

A body-worn hearing aid may be more powerful (capable of making the sound louder) than a behind-the-ear (post-aural) aid.

Body-worn aids should be worn clipped to the **outside** of a breast pocket on the child's shirt or blouse. If the child does not have pockets he should wear a simple harness for it. Children need to be encouraged to wear their aid like this as they often want to hide them (perhaps in their trouser pocket) so that they look like other children. This stops the receiver from making useful sounds louder for the child. It will make the noise of cloth of the pocket rubbing loud instead – **not very useful**.

HEARING AIDS IN TROUSER POCKETS OR LEFT AT HOME OR WITH NO BATTERY ARE NO GOOD AT ALL – HEARING AIDS MUST BE WORN AND MUST BE FUNCTIONING.

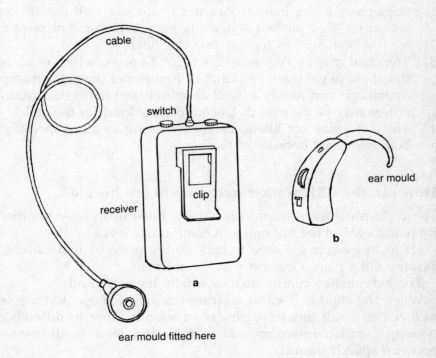

Body worn (a) and post-aural (b) hearing aids

How does a deaf child learn to use his aid?

1. The child should have been given his aid after a careful assessment of his hearing.
2. He should have been given an earmould which has been especially made to be comfortable for his ears. He will need a separate mould for each ear.
3. He and his family should also have been given instruction in how to use the aid.

This may not have happened so what should the CBR worker know?

Problems

Some of the problems the child may have with his hearing aid are:

1. That the aid makes background noise louder and this may be very unpleasant for the child who has become used to a rather quiet world.
2. The ear mould may be uncomfortable with rough pieces which can be filed down or maybe it just does not fit comfortably. Sometimes if the mould does not fit the ear well the aid will give off a high pitched squeaking noise which is not pleasant for the deaf child or for any one else nearby.
3. The child may be very sensitive to loud noises (which reach his threshold of pain, see Section 2.1). Remember the aid will amplify background noises as well as speech and these background noises may be very loud. Uncomfortably loud for the child.
4. The child may not like to be seen wearing an aid, especially a body-worn aid because of teasing.

How can the CBR worker help him to use his aid?

The child must learn to put his aid on, must learn how to switch it on and control the volume to a comfortable level.

He must learn to get used to background noise by first using his aid in a quiet place for short periods of time.

The aid must be comfortable especially the earmould.

When the child is used to wearing the aid he must slowly learn to listen to small (fine) differences of sounds. First to differences between similar environmental sounds and later to differences between speech sounds.

He must learn to look after his aid.

How to look after an aid

Check the battery. Does it fit? Is it still working? Are the spare batteries in good condition? How are they being stored? Where can you get a regular supply of batteries? Are they expensive? Can the family afford them?

Keeping the ear piece (earmould) clean. The ear piece should be taken off the cable or tube and washed regularly, use a pin to gently clear any wax from the canal, dry the mould in the sun, attach it back on to the cable or tube.

Often the cable of a body worn aid breaks, especially at the point where it joins the ear piece. If there is someone in the village or community who is skilled with a soldering iron he may be able to make a simple repair to the cable.

Sometimes the tube joining the aid to the earpiece of a behind-the-ear aid splits. If there is enough tube left, or if you have a supply, cut off the split piece with a clean cut and refit the earpiece.

With small children it is important to make sure that the microphone of a body-worn aid does not become blocked with food. If it does it can be carefully cleaned making sure it does not get wet. It is also possible to fit a microphone cover. You can buy these or make one from the very fine mesh perhaps from an old tea strainer. The mesh lets the sound through but not particles of food.

If other things go wrong or if the child needs a new earpiece you will have to contact the centre.

PART 3

Children with Mental Handicap
(Learning Disorders)

SECTION 3.1

What is mental handicap?

Mental handicap occurs when a person has a much lower intelligence than normal, and this affects the way in which he learns and adapts to his environment. He functions generally at a simple childlike level and will probably need help and support all his life. He will find learning skills and making relationships more difficult than a child who is not mentally handicapped. Because he finds learning difficult, many people do not use the term **mental handicap** but prefer to say that the child has **learning difficulties**.

A child who is mentally handicapped will develop at a much slower rate than other children of the same age. He will probably be slower at all his developmental milestones or stages (smiling, sitting, crawling, walking, feeding himself, toilet training and talking).

Normally children learn a great deal from what goes on around them. They watch, imitate, play and learn. They do this partly for themselves and partly with help from older children and adults who play with them. They like to play with other people, to interact and be social right from the time they are babies. They seem to want to learn and are interested in new things, new people and new situations. They remember things that have happened before, use the knowledge they remember and go on and extend or develop it by trying new ideas that they get from new situations.

The mentally handicapped child does not behave like this. He may not play at all, or just a very little. If he does play, he may do the same things over and over again, and show no interest in changing to new activities, new things or people. He may seem not to learn by watching and imitating things around him. He may seem not to be interested in people and responding to them. He may even seem not to notice anything that is happening around him. He may, however, smile and look happy, watch what is going on, but show no understanding of it and no memory that the same things have happened before. The activities that are going on around him have little or no meaning for him. He can't make any sense of them, because his brain is not developing fully.

While the mentally handicapped child often shows delay in gross motor development, it is in the fields of learning, communicating and social behaviour that his disabilities are most obvious. The child develops these skills as he grows, and it is therefore not always immediately obvious at an early stage, that he is mentally handicapped. This is particularly true if he is only mildly affected.

As with other disabilities, people can be very severely affected or just mildly affected. If the child is badly affected, he may not be able to learn very much at all. Perhaps only feeding and dressing himself and some very basic communication skills like answering 'yes' and 'no', and indicating some basic needs like hunger. If the child is only mildly affected, he should be capable of learning a great many skills for living and communicating and can become fairly independent. Whether he does this or not, depends very much on the way he is looked after, generally encouraged to learn and the methods used to teach him specific skills.

A structured teaching programme, aimed at the child's level and which is highly relevant to his needs, is felt to be the most successful approach to his development. By aiming at the level of the child, the programme is building on what the child knows and has already achieved, and is reinforcing and extending that knowledge. See earlier in this section for a brief description of how the normal child learns. The programme should be relevant (useful) to the child. This is always true, but particularly so, in mental handicap because the child's ability to learn is limited and therefore any effort the child makes to learn should be in learning skills that he is going to use a lot.

It is therefore important to identify the child's needs and plan a structured, consistent programme to help him. This should be done with everyone who spends time with him, e.g. his parents, his brothers and sisters, his CBR worker and school, if he goes to one.

It is the people who know him best, who know what he can do and what will be most useful for him to learn. It is important that all these people do the same things, in the same way with him, as this makes learning much easier. If everyone does different things, in different ways it may confuse him and make it more difficult for him to learn.

Task analysis

A good method of teaching skills in a simple way is by **task analysis**. This method consists of identifying a skill to teach and then breaking it down into small steps that the child can achieve fairly easily. This means that the child is rewarded by frequent success and can build up the skill step by step. If the task becomes too difficult, it is possible to drop back a step to one that the child can do and move up again when the child is more sure of his ability to achieve the next step. This prevents the child from failing and possibly giving up because he feels it is too difficult and he can't do it. He is rewarded by achieving small parts of the task and eventually building it into a successful whole task, instead of trying the whole task and failing to achieve it, giving up and feeling that he can't do it.

An example of task analysis

A child knows when he wants a drink, but can't ask for it. He shouts and screams in the same way as he does when he wants a biscuit or a toy. He always has a drink in the same cup and knows it is a drink. It is decided that the skill to teach is for him to have a word or sound that is recognised by everyone for drink. This word or sound must only mean drink. The cup will be a useful way of helping him achieve this. He will point to the cup if you say 'where is the drink?'

To encourage the child to try and learn, it is a good idea to reinforce or reward his attempts at achieving the task. Success in learning something is a very good reinforcer or reward, but it often helps the child if he gets an extra reward as well. Lots of people use sweets for this, but anything that the child likes and is special can be used e.g. going for a swim in the sea, going to the shop or market, building a pile of stones or bricks and counting how many at the end of the game.

The **target skill** (what we want to achieve at the end of the programme) in this case is saying 'drink' or a recognisable sound that means drink whenever he says it.

In the process of reaching this target skill the child will progress through various steps of learning:

1. Will point to lots of different cups when asked 'where is the drink?'
2. Will attempt to imitate 'drink' when you point to the cup and say 'what is this?'.

3. Will say 'drink' when you point to the cup and give him the initial sound cue of 'd'.
4. Will say 'drink' when you point to the cup.
5. Will spontaneously say 'drink' when shown the cup.
6. Will spontaneously say and use 'drink' to obtain a drink.

This is just an example of the kind of progression it is possible to use to teach a skill. The child's level of skill and learning ability and style will influence how many steps it is necessary to use and how much reinforcement is necessary on one step before moving on to the next.

THE MENTALLY HANDICAPPED CHILD IS SLOW AT LEARNING BUT BY IDENTIFYING HIS NEEDS AND STRUCTURING AN APPROPRIATE TEACHING PROGRAMME FOR HIM, IT IS POSSIBLE TO TEACH HIM MANY NEW SKILLS, INCLUDING COMMUNICATION.

Questions

Section 3.1 What is mental handicap?

1.	Mentally handicapped children will grow into normal adults.	True/False	**Marks:** 1
2.	Delay in gross motor development is the most noticeable sign of mental handicap.	True/False	**Marks:** 1
3.	Communication is usually affected in mental handicap.	True/False	**Marks:** 1
4.	Mentally handicapped children are slow to learn.	True/False	**Marks:** 1
5.	Name three ways normal children learn.		**Marks:** 3
6.	Mentally handicapped children will learn everything normal children learn.	True/False	**Marks:** 1
7.	Name four factors that are important in planning a teaching programme for mentally handicapped children.		**Marks:** 4
8.	The teaching programme should be carried out by one person only.	True/False	**Marks:** 1
9.	Name four factors that are important for making Task Analysis a good teaching method for the mentally handicapped.		**Marks:** 4
10.	Name three areas of development that are most affected by mental handicap.		**Marks:** 3

SECTION 3.2

How can we help a slow child to develop language?

We learnt in Section 1.1 that communication:

- is social,
- can be verbal and non-verbal,
- has lots of different methods,
- is two-way,
- can be used for lots of different reasons or functions.

In Section 1.2 we learnt how communication normally develops. Mentally handicapped or slow children develop communication in the same way as normal children, but they progress more slowly and need more stimulation and help from other people to help them learn.

We all communicate so easily, that we don't think about how complicated and difficult the communication process is. The child has to listen, understand the message he hears, decide what he is going to say in reply and say it. Because the mentally handicapped child's brain hasn't developed fully, he finds this a difficult process. If the message is long, complicated or about something that is not in front of him, it is more difficult for him.

One way in which we can help the slow child is to be very careful about how we talk to him. Most people quite naturally use a simple form of speech to talk to children. You might like to think about the way you talk to friends and people you work with, and compare that with the way you might talk to a child. There are lots of differences. Your friends would be very surprised if you started to talk to them in the slightly higher pitched and louder voice you use to talk to children. You also use short, simple sentences with lots of emphasis on the words that are important, so that the child can easily pick out the words that carry the message, e.g. 'Give me the **ball**', 'Here's your **drink**'.

It is very important that we talk to slow learning children in a simple way. So remember to:

1. Make it quite clear what you are talking about, by using more than one method of communication, e.g. use words and gestures: 'Here's your drink' – point to the drink, and possibly demonstrate drinking.
2. Use short, simple sentences.
3. Use common, easy words that the child will understand easily and that will be useful to him.
4. Use a slightly louder voice than you would usually use.
5. Say the important words with more force, so that the child can pick them out easily.
6. Speak a little slower than usual.
7. Give plenty of time for the child to understand the message and make a reply.

A practical way to encourage the development of communication is to do things together with the child and talk about it. Sharing an activity, a game, work, shopping, going out to visit a friend, is a very real way to learn language. The language means something there and then and is real. This should be completely natural and happen all the time. As an adult you say the word the child is trying to say correctly and you are therefore a **'model'** for the right communication, you can **reinforce** what the child says by responding and repeating it, and you **extend** and **develop** his knowledge by adding to and expanding the communication. For example, the child and his mother are in the street, the child sees a car and points at it, turns to his mother and says, 'Ta, der ta'. Mummy says, 'Yes, it's a car, a red car. Would you like to go in a car?'. The child's mother is responding, reinforcing, modelling and expanding the child's original communication. She is responding by replying to the child and saying 'Yes'. She is reinforcing what the child has said by repeating it and replying to him. She is modelling the right communication by saying the word correctly, although it is important not to tell the child he is wrong. Just say it correctly, so he can hear how the word should be said. She is expanding what he is saying by giving him some more information about the car.

This mother is modelling, reinforcing and expanding

THE BEST AND MOST EFFECTIVE WAY TO LEARN TO COMMUNICATE IS IN REAL SITUATIONS.

Always respond

Always respond to the child's attempts at communicating, even when you are unsure of what he is saying. If you don't respond, it will discourage the child from trying to communicate. It is important to make every effort to understand what the child is talking about, because your reply will keep the interaction and conversation going. This is obviously easier if you can guess what the child is talking about from the situation. If the child is very difficult to understand, always respond when he tries to communicate. You can always make opportunities to have a conversation in a situation when you can probably guess what he is saying. This means that you can respond with more than 'mmmm' and give him a real reply. Mealtimes or when you are playing a game with him would be a good time for real situations like this.

Don't talk for him

Avoid talking for the child. Try to give him opportunities to communicate himself. He should try to communicate even when it is difficult, or takes a long time. Help him out if he gets totally stuck or encourage him to help himself. He could do this by using another method of communication like gestures or saying it another way, instead of just repeating the same message. Help him but **don't do it for him**. Communicating for him could make him very passive, quiet and unwilling to communicate.

Expect him to communicate

Expect the child to communicate. Be ready to receive his communication and respond to it. He is probably communicating more than you think. Learn to recognise his efforts at communication, even if they are not all spoken. Remember that there are lots of different methods of communication and although we usually communicate by speaking, we can use other methods. Respond to them all.

Follow the child's lead

Take your lead from the child. Look for situations where the child is interested and really seems to want something very badly. He will be much more motivated to learn if it is something that is really important to him.

Time to respond

Give the child time to respond when you ask him a question or you are having a conversation. The slow learning child may take some time to listen, understand, decide on his answer and communicate it to you. **You must wait for him**. If you don't it may make him give up trying and become passive and silent.

Use every possible opportunity to encourage the child to communicate. Make it fun and rewarding for him so that he wants to go on communicating.

Questions

Section 3.2 How can we help a slow child to develop language.

1.	Communication is difficult for the slow learning child because his brain is not fully developed.	True/False	**Marks:** 1
2.	Name three things the child needs to do before he can reply to your question.		**Marks:** 3
3.	Name five ways that we can make what we say to slow learning children simple.		**Marks:** 5
4.	You should only respond to the child's communication when it is easy to understand.	True/False	**Marks:** 1
5.	A child who does not respond, has not understood.	True/False	**Marks:** 1
6.	The only communication that should be accepted is speech.	True/False	**Marks:** 1
7.	Name three roles you have as an adult when communicating with a child.		**Marks:** 3
8.	Communication is only taught at school.	True/False	**Marks:** 1
9.	Helping the child to communicate by talking for him is a good idea.	True/False	**Marks:** 1
10.	Teach the child the words you think he should know.	True/False	**Marks:** 1
11.	Name two differences between the way that you talk to your friends and the way that you talk to children.		**Marks:** 2

Skills

Section 3.2 How can we help a slow child to develop language?

Activity 1

Spend some time with a mentally handicapped child and his parents. Observe the interaction and communication that is going on between them.

Help them to help their child by showing them how they can make language simpler for their child to understand. (See Section 3.2, pages 60 and 61.) Do this by making them notice what they are doing.

Stop them after an interaction with the child and go back over the communication they were using and the way the child was responding.

You should make sure they understand about: **short, simple sentences**. Take one of their own sentences as an example and show them how they could say the same thing in a much simpler way. e.g. Parent says,

'Okay Johnny, it's a really nice day, the sun is shining and it's hot, so when you've finished drinking your milk and playing with your toys, we'll put them away and walk down to the market and buy some bananas.'

You could demonstrate that an easier way to say the same thing would be: 'Johnny, when you've finished, we'll go and buy some bananas.'

The rest of the sentence the parent said is either not necessary to the meaning or understood without actually saying the words.

If you wanted to tell Johnny more, it would be easier to break it into short sentences, so that he could understand it in small lumps. A long, sentence with lots of information is very difficult to understand in one go. This would be easier: 'Johnny, it's a hot, sunny day. – When you've finished your drink, we'll put your toys away. – Then we could go out. – We could go to the market and buy some bananas.'

Remind them to:

- Talk slowly, and demonstrate so they really understand.
- Say the words that are really important with more force, so that they are noticed and remembered.
- Always respond to the child's communication.
- Leave time for the child to reply.

You should practise these skills with them, and then leave them to practise with their child.

Go back after a week and look for improvement in everyday conversation.

Repeat the process, using the parent–child interaction as the teaching material. Help them see where they have been using the new skills and praise them for it. Then point out where they are not using simple communication, and demonstrate ways in which they could make it short and simple to understand.

Activity 2

Teach the parent of a mentally handicapped child about the three roles they have as an adult helping a child with communication. (Modelling the correct communication, reinforcing what the child has said, and expanding what he has said.) Look back to Section 3.2, page 61, to remind you. They might be doing this already, but if you show them what they are doing and explain why it is important, they can do it on purpose to help their child at all times, instead of just by chance, sometimes.

As in Activity 1, it is best to listen and observe what is being said between the child and the parent. Use that to either show them how good they are at **modelling**, **reinforcing**, and **expanding**, or to show them places in the conversation where they could improve.

Demonstrate or model the process for them, and practise it with them. Then ask them to practise with their child.

As in Activity 1, go back after a week and look for improvement in everyday conversation.

Repeat the exercise, using their conversation with their child as teaching material. Help them see where they have been **modelling**, **reinforcing** and **expanding** and praise them. Then point out where they could have used the modelling, reinforcing and expanding process. Demonstrate ways they could do this.

Activity 3

Do a *task analysis* with the parent of a slow learning child. Look back at Section 3.1, page 58, to remind you of the way a task analysis is done.

1. Identify the skill that you want to teach the child together.

2. Agree on what his present behaviour is and think about how you are going to reach the target skill in 1.

3. Now break down the target skill into logical, small steps that the child can achieve one at a time. Write these down and number them.

4. Decide on the number of times a day you are going to teach the skill.

5. Decide on the reinforcers you will use for succeeding at a step. Success is one sort of reinforcer, but are you going to use other ones?

Example of chart for task analysis

Day	1	2	3	4	5
Whole task					
Verbal prompt					
Simple physical prompt					
Big physical prompt					

Whole Task – child calling Daddy by name 'Daddy'

Verbal Prompt – adult saying 'Daddy, here's Daddy. You say it.'

Simple Physical Prompt – adult points at Daddy and says 'Daddy, here's Daddy. Who's this?'

Big Physical Prompt – adult takes child's hand and touches Daddy with it. Adult says 'This is Daddy. Look, here's Daddy. Who's this? You say it. Tell me who it is.'

6. Teach the skill. Start at Step 1. Move on to Step 2 when Step 1 has been achieved. If you move on too fast and the child fails, drop back to the previous step and only move on when you feel the child can attempt the next step.

7. Mark off each stage as the child achieves it. This is very helpful for the parent because even when the step is very small, progress can be seen.

How to use the chart for Task Analysis

1. Always try the Whole Task first. It may be that the child finds it easy to imitate. Try the Whole Task two or three times before moving down to the first prompt (clue) – Verbal Prompt.

2. Try the task with the Verbal Prompt two or three times. If the child succeeds, repeat the task with the Verbal Prompt about five times and then attempt it without the Verbal Prompt – the Whole Task. The child will probably succeed at the Whole Task now, but if not you can always go back to the Verbal Prompt.

Example of chart for task analysis

Day	1	2	3	4	5
Whole task	X X X		X X X	X ✓ ✓ ✓ ✓	✓ ✓ ✓ ✓ ✓ ✓
Verbal prompt	X X		✓ ✓ ✓ ✓ ✓ ✓ ✓	✓ ✓ ✓	
Simple physical prompt	X X	X ✓ ✓ ✓ ✓ ✓	✓ ✓		
Big physical prompt	X X ✓ ✓ ✓ ✓ ✓	✓ ✓			

Whole Task – child calling Daddy by name 'Daddy'

Verbal Prompt – adult saying 'Daddy, here's Daddy. You say it.'

Simple Physical Prompt – adult points at Daddy and says 'Daddy, here's Daddy. Who's this?'

Big Physical Prompt – adult takes child's hand and touches Daddy with it. Adult says 'This is Daddy. Look, here's Daddy. Who's this? You say it. Tell me who it is.'

3. If the child fails, move down a step to the Simple Physical Prompt. Follow the same instructions as for the Verbal Prompt, depending on whether the child succeeds or fails at the Simple Physical Prompt level.

4. Move up and down the four levels of difficulty:
   - Whole Task
   - Verbal Prompt
   - Simple Physical Prompt
   - Big Physical Prompt

   depending on how the child is doing.

5. Each time the child fails an attempt at the task put a cross on the chart in the right square. Each time the child succeeds at the task, put a tick.

6. The right square is the one for the day and level you are working at. See the worked example for the child saying Daddy. This chart has only 5 days on it, but you can have as many as you like.

7. You are aiming to get the task right each time. Then you can move up a step. Remember the Whole Task is the hardest and the task with the Big Physical Prompt is the easiest.

SECTION 3.3

How can we help a very mentally handicapped child to communicate?

Pre-verbal skills

We saw in Section 1.2 how communication develops, and how there is a lot of communication before speech. This is called pre-verbal communication. It consists of:

- cries,
- sounds,
- gestures,
- a combination of sounds and gestures,
- listening,
- imitating,
- attending together, and
- turn-taking.

Learning to use these skills is not only very imporant for basic communication before speech develops but it also forms a framework for verbal language. Children who do not learn to listen and take turns in conversation become very poor communicators. They miss part of what is said to them, because they don't listen and if they do not understand about taking turns they cannot control the sending of messages and the listening to messages. (You will remember from Section 1 that everybody both sends and listens and responds to messages.)

Turn-taking allows the child to change quickly from the role of listener to sender. This skill is very important for good communication.

For all pre-verbal skills it is important to remember to:

1. Involve the child in what you do. Share activities with him. Turn it into a game if possible – so that it is fun and he will want to do it again.

2. Give the child time to respond.
3. Encourage and respond to any communication he makes.
4. Repeat activities frequently. Children like favourite activities to be repeated over and over again. They need the practice. They will quicky tell you when they are bored and then you should stop.
5. Don't force the child if he really does not want to do something.
6. Do activities with the child when he is awake and alert and full of energy. It will be much more successful than trying to make a tired child do things.
7. Take your lead from the child – do things he is interested in. You cannot force him to do anything, you can only encourage and give him lots of opportunities.

BE VERY PATIENT. HE CANNOT BE LIKE OTHER CHILDREN.

Attending together

Encourage attending together, by being physically close to the child and having time to watch and look and also explore things by touch and smell. You feel something, e.g. a fruit, and then give it to the child to do the same. Then you repeat the action or smell it too and

Attending together

let the child do the same. Looking at pictures or books is a good joint activity. You can talk about the pictures too. Doing jobs around the house can be shared activities. The child can watch you peel the vegetables and then can feel them and play with them, with and without the skin on. You can talk to him about the skin and taking it off. How you take the skin off, why you take the skin off. What is happening to the vegetables next, and so on. You could go and see where the vegetables grow or where you buy them. You are using the vegetables to attend together.

The child will soon learn to attract your attention by using something like a toy or activity. He might bring you something or point at something that he is interested in. He is requesting that you look at the things together, and you should respond by doing just that. He is beginning to learn that he can get what he wants (in this case your attention) by communicating.

In your busy day, make sure there is some special time when you can respond like this.

Imitating

The skill of imitating is very important for learning generally, but particularly for learning language. Children imitate sounds and spoken language, and practise it until it sounds like the words they can hear around them.

Imitating starts with copying activities, like rolling a ball, giving you something, putting a hat on and taking it off, putting dolly to bed. Children imitate real life activities too, such as shopping, cleaning the house, washing the dishes and combing your hair. As you play you can introduce noises into the game for the child to imitate. He may imitate 'moo' for a cow or 'woof' for a dog, 'brrm, brrm' for a car etc. Here he is not only imitating the activity and the sound, but he is linking them together, so that they mean something. This is a very important step for him as if he says 'moo', everyone knows he means cow. If he says 'brrm brrm', we know he means car. Sometimes these sounds turn into the child's first words and he uses them for a few years to mean cow and car. They can be called first words because each sound has a special meaning and only means that one thing.

To encourage imitation, start with actions or sounds that you know the child can do and gradually make them more complicated. Make sure he is watching and encourage him by saying something like 'you have a go' or 'you try'. Help him either physically, by moving his hands or verbally with or without a demonstration

Imitating

Turn-taking

depending how much help he needs. Always accept any efforts he makes in attempting to do the task. Think back to Task Analysis (Section 3.1) and reward the steps.

Turn-taking

Turn-taking is the basis for conversation and like the other skills we have talked about here it is developed long before words are used. Encouraging the child to take turns should be done with an activity that the child likes. As with **imitating**, make sure he is watching and attending to the activity. To begin with it is helpful to say 'your turn', 'my turn' when the time comes to change turns. Help him if necessary by demonstrating the action, physically helping him to do the action, telling him what to do, or a combination of all three. Give him less and less help as he gets better at taking turns.

All sorts of activities can be used for basic turn-taking practice. Cuddles and kisses can be given in turns. First Mummy and then the child. Turns can be taken in patting a ball or a balloon; clapping hands; pushing each other over; building a tower of bricks – you put one brick on and the child puts the next one on; putting things in a box – the child puts one in and you put the next in and so on. Lots of everyday activities can have turns – shopping, taking turns to put things in the bag, cooking, taking turns to put spoonfuls of rice in a bowl etc. These are just a few ideas. You will be able to think of lots more.

Further development

Into the framework of **attending together**, **imitation** and **taking turns** the child will begin to add sounds. We began to think about this earlier in this section where we talked about imitating animal noises and car noises. He will begin to produce more and more sounds that are sometimes linked to a gesture, but are always identifiable as meaning one thing like 'moo' for cow. It may be less obvious, like 'der' meaning 'daddy'. One child we knew said 'da' for yes for years. The important point is that the sound used for meaning something is always the same. If talking is difficult for the child, he may continue to use sounds and gestures for a long time. There is nothing wrong with this, as he is still communicating and is still able to use his communication for many different functions: e.g., greetings can be sounds and gestures; simple requests can be sounds and gestures – holding out a cup and making a sound might always mean 'drink'. Pointing at the door and making a particular sound might always mean 'I want to go out'.

'Yes' and 'no' are usually able to be recognised by sounds and gestures. Looking unhappy and crying might mean that the child was unhappy. His mother might be able to recognise the emotion,

eat food   drink   sleep

good   baby   house/home

up   down   me/I

you   big   small

These examples show how a sign language can be built by expanding the natural gestures people make. A system like this has been developed by the Makaton Vocabulary Development Project. More information can be obtained from them. (The address can be found on page 104.)

but with communication skills that only consisted of gestures and sounds it would probably be difficult to find out why the child was unhappy.

Developing more language

To express more complicated ideas and emotions it is necessary to develop a more sophisticated language of words and rules. Lots of slow learning children will find this very difficult and may never progress past gestures and sounds and a few single words. These children should be encouraged to use all the methods of communication that they can to help them send their message. They often find sign language, an expanded gesture system, very helpful. This is useful for them to do and to watch people do as the message they see lasts longer than the message they hear.

Progress

If the child is going to progress to words and linking words, the ideas in the previous Section (3.2) would apply. Also see Section 1.2 about normally developing language.

Questions

Section 3.3   How we can help a very mentally handicapped child to communicate?

1.	Making sounds and using gestures are two pre-verbal skills. Name four others.		**Marks:** 4
2.	Attending together is just being physically close.	True/False	**Marks:** 1
3.	Give three examples of activities that encourage attending together.		**Marks:** 3
4.	Activities are imitated, speech is not.	True/False	**Marks:** 1
5.	Give three examples of activities that encourage imitation.		**Marks:** 3
6.	Turn-taking is about playing card games.	True/False	**Marks:** 1
7.	Give three examples of activities which encourage turn-taking.		**Marks:** 3
8.	Name four functions of communication that can be used with basic gestures and sounds.		**Marks:** 4

Skills

Section 3.3   How can we help a very mentally handicapped child to communicate?

Activity 1: Encouraging attending together

Observe a mentally handicapped child with his parent. Decide what sort of things seem to interest him. Talk to his parent about using things that seem to interest him to encourage him to attend and therefore learn. Remember:
- to choose something you think will interest the child,
- take your lead from the child,
- don't force the child, and
- give the child time to learn.

Demonstrate to the parent how this can be done. Use objects and people to gain the child's attention and then talk to him about the object or person that interested him. The parent should then try to copy the process you've shown them, using different objects.

Note down when the child uses the same process to gain the attention of you or his parent, e.g. noises, looking, pushing and pulling, pointing, waving etc.

Help the parent to notice this too. The parent needs to recognise the child's **attending together** message and respond to it always. Watch the child and parent playing together and help her notice the child's attempts at communication.

Activity 2: Encouraging imitation

Activities

Observe a very mentally handicapped child with his parent. Decide what sort of activities and play he seems to like doing. Decide with his mother that you are going to try and get him to copy or imitate some simple activities.

The activities you decide on will depend on his age, level of development, the observation you've done and the discussion with his mother. Remember:
- to choose something you think the child will like,
- take your lead from the child,
- don't force the child,
- give the child time to learn – lots of repetition.

Choose about four different activities to try with him. If the child does not imitate the whole task immediately, try giving him a verbal prompt. If this fails, give him a simple physical prompt and if this fails help him more by giving him a big physical prompt. Here are some examples. If he is at an early development level, try:

1. Building a tower of bricks in front of him and knocking it down.
    - Build it again and see if he will knock it down – whole task imitation.
    - If after a few chances to imitate the whole task he fails to do so, give him a verbal prompt like 'you knock it down, come on like this' and show him.
    - If this fails after a few chances, give him a simple physical prompt by guiding his hand to the tower.
    - If this fails give him a big physical prompt by guiding his hand and helping him knock it over.
    - Do this with him until he feels confident enough to knock it over himself after having his hand guided. When he can do that, just give him a verbal prompt. From there he should be able to progress to imitating the whole task by himself.
2. Putting objects in a box.
    - You do it a few times, making sure he's watching you.
    - If he does not copy you, try telling him what to do – 'you put this in the box' – a verbal prompt.
    - If that doesn't work, try giving him the object – a simple physical prompt.
    - If that does not work, give him the object and guide his hand into the box – a big physical prompt.
    - Like the first example, give him less help, as he begins to understand what to do.
3. Cover your head or his head with a cloth and then remove it and play peekaboo.

Use the same procedure as with the other activities, helping him if necessary and then gradually taking the help away.

Write down for each activity:

1. How many demonstrations it took before the child would imitate the activity with some prompting.
2. How many demonstrations it took before the child would imitate the activity without any prompting.

After he had learnt to imitate, did he learn more quickly. Discuss with his parent lots of different activities that could be used like this. The activities should use the four sorts of prompts where necessary:
- whole task imitation,
- verbal prompt,
- simple physical prompt,
- big physical prompt.

Sounds

Do exactly the same procedure for speech sounds.

Linking

Use the same sort of procedure for linking sounds to objects like cars and animals. See Section 3.3.

Activity 3: Encouraging taking turns

Lots of the activities you do for imitation can be extended into turn-taking activities.

Games

When the child has learnt some imitation skill, turn the activity into turn-taking by suggesting turns are taken. e.g. If you are building a brick tower or putting objects into a box, or banging with a hammer, take it in turns. You do one and then offer the child a brick or object and say 'your turn'. Then you do one and say 'my turn'. Continue like this until the child understands what to do. You can then take away the verbal prompt of 'your turn, my turn'.

Discuss with the parent lots of different activities that can be used like this.

Try and encourage the parent to make turn-taking games out of things they do every day.

Songs and rhymes

Finishing off songs, stories and rhymes is another sort of turn-taking activity. You say part of the song, rhyme or story and the child can finish it.

As with the previous activities, notice when the child starts to say something – song, end of a story or rhyme – and finish it for him. Help the parent to notice when this is happening, so that they can respond. Help them to become very aware of this so they can always respond.

Do this by demonstrating for them, practising with them and observing what they do. Help them to recognise when they are responding at the right time and when they have failed to respond to the child.

Encouragement

Encourage parents to keep turn-taking activities going. The chain of interactions should go on for lots of turns. This is important for non-verbal activities such as the games we have been talking about, and for conversations. It is therefore important that parents know how to talk to their child in a simple way. See Section 3.2 for ideas and how to encourage the conversation.

Discuss with the parents of a mentally handicapped child ways of helping the child to communicate. You might like to consider:
● time to respond,
● saying the message in a different way.

· Look back through this book and find some other ideas and think of at least two new ideas for keeping the conversation going, even if the conversation consists mainly of sounds and gestures.

Remember to demonstrate, then observe the parent and child, and use the observation to help them see what they are doing.

SECTION 3.4

Can we help a mentally handicapped child go to school?

Schools for mentally handicapped children

There are, of course, special schools for mentally handicapped children. These are often known as 'schools for children with learning difficulties'.

The advantages of a good special school are that:

1. The child will be with children who have similar difficulties to himself.
2. He will be taught by specially trained teachers who know how to help such children.
3. The school curriculum and school organisation will be appropriate for the child's needs.

The disadvantages of special schools for some families are that:

1. They can be a long way from home.
2. They can be expensive.
3. They may use a language not used by the child and his family.

How can the mentally handicapped child learn?

The first answer to this question has to be that he can learn a lot. The important point to recognise is that although a mentally handicapped child cannot become like a normal child, he can learn:

- self-help skills (looking after his own needs),
- social behaviour,
- to do tasks, crafts or jobs, and
- communication skills.

He will achieve these objectives best at a special school.

Can a mentally handicapped child go to the village school?

The answer to this question is maybe. The answer will depend on a lot of factors. For example:

1. How handicapped the child is – it is easier for a slightly handicapped child to mix into the village school than a very handicapped child.
2. Whether he has other handicaps: if he is mobile, strong and healthy it is much easier to integrate him into the village school than if he has physical problems and/or mobility problems or deafness or blindness as well as his mental handicap.
3. The attitude of the village teacher – if the teacher is not willing to accept the child, there is little the CBR worker can do. The CBR worker can try to explain how to help the child. To explain how important it is for the child to have the opportunity of some schooling and the chance to mix with other children. The CBR worker can offer to support the teacher.

Development of communication skills

The rest of this chapter will concentrate on how the mentally handicapped child's communication skills can be developed at school. The problems of integrating the mentally handicapped child into a village school and developing his communication skills are similar in many ways to the integration of deaf children which was discussed in Section 2.4.

Before deciding if the mentally handicapped child can go to school, it is important to consider the factors listed above and to consider his communication skills.

Before the possibility of integrating the mentally handicapped child into school is even considered, he will need to have developed:

1. Good communication skills so that he can make his wants known.
2. Some understanding skills so that he understands instructions.
3. Confidence to use his language skills.

Let us consider these points in a little more detail.

1. The mentally handicapped child needs to be able to tell someone if he wants to go to the lavatory, if he needs a new pencil, if he is hurt, that he has not finished his task etc.
2. He needs to be able to understand the teacher if he is to benefit at all from school. A mentally handicapped child will probably

understand less than a healthy child most of the time. If the mentally handicapped child understands nothing of what is going on in the classroom, there is little point in him being there at all. This will be especially true if the other children know that he does not understand things and tease and mock him because of this. If he does not understand or if he is teased he may become disruptive (behave badly) in the classroom, or he may become very withdrawn.

3. It is important that the mentally handicapped child has enough confidence to use his communication skills and not be shy or frightened by the other children in the class.

If the child has few of the additional problems listed on page 80 and has the communication skills listed above, and if the village teacher is willing to accept him, then it may be possible for him to manage to cope in a village school.

How can the CBR worker help the village teacher to help the mentally handicapped child?

If the village teacher is willing to have the mentally handicapped child in his school, there are certain things which the CBR worker can do to make it a little easier for the teacher and the child.

The CBR worker can help the teacher to understand something of mental handicap. If the teacher understands that the child:

- cannot understand as easily as other children,
- may be rather clumsy,
- may have unclear speech,
- may be very forgetful, etc.,

then he is less likely to beat the child because he thinks the child is naughty. Beating the mentally handicapped child is likely to make his behaviour worse not better. If the CBR worker can help the teacher understand this it will be a great help.

It will be quite difficult for the teacher to manage the mentally handicapped child in a busy classroom and it may be that the CBR worker can either help in the classroom once a week herself or find a village woman who would be able to help the teacher with the child in the classroom on a regular basis. Such a person could be trained by the CBR worker about some of the problems of mental handicap and then work with the teacher to help the child with the work the teacher has given him.

PART 4

Cerebral Palsy

SECTION 4.1

What is cerebral palsy and how does it affect communication?

Cerebral palsy is the name given to a large number of disorders which are caused by brain damage before birth, at birth or just after birth.

The disorders are similar because:

1. The brain damage affects movement and posture.
2. The brain damage itself does not change or get worse.
3. **But**, the symptoms, i.e. the problems with movement may change and/or get worse.
4. The brain damage may also affect:
   - vision,
   - hearing,
   - speech,
   - thinking and language,
   - touch sensation.

Cerebral palsy affects speech because speech depends on movement and control of muscles in the face, mouth and neck. These muscles will be affected by the cerebral palsy in the same way as arm and leg muscles are. Movement will be slow and uncoordinated or jerky. This will make speech slow, uncoordinated and jerky.

Cerebral palsy also affects breathing. Breath is needed to make voice. Poor muscle control can mean not breathing very deeply, so not much breath is taken in. Therefore there is not much breath to breathe out and make voice.

This means that voice comes in short bursts. Voice is used to make speech so speech comes in short bursts. Therefore speech is jerky, uncoordinated and produced in single words or very short phrases.

Some cerebral palsied children may be so very severely affected that they have not enough control to speak at all. They are non-verbal children.

This does not necessarily mean that they are stupid, cannot or do not want to communicate. They have to learn to communicate in different ways.

Cerebral palsy may cause the child to be slow at learning, but this is not always true. Difficulties in talking do not necessarily mean difficulties in thinking.

If talking is very difficult the cerebral palsied child should be encouraged to use other ways of communicating to help him communicate and help others understand him. For example,

- gestures,
- pointing, looking,
- pictures,
- facial expression, and
- sounds.

Show me what you want.

A child using a communication board

Questions

Section 4.1 What is cerebral palsy and how does it affect communication?

1.	Cerebral palsy is the name of one disorder.	True/False	**Marks:**	1
2.	Cerebral palsy is caused by brain damage.	True/False	**Marks:**	1
3.	The brain damage changes as the child develops.	True/False	**Marks:**	1
4.	The brain damage mainly affects movement.	True/False	**Marks:**	1
5.	Name five other aspects of development that may be affected by cerebral palsy.		**Marks:**	5
6.	Cerebral palsy does not affect communication.	True/False	**Marks:**	1
7.	Speech involves movements of muscles in the — — —. Name three places.		**Marks:**	3
8.	All children with cerebral palsy can learn to talk.	True/False	**Marks:**	1
9.	Name five ways, (apart from speech) that cerebral palsied children can use to communicate.		**Marks:**	5
10.	Cerebral palsied children always have learning difficulties.	True/False	**Marks:**	1

Skills

Section 4.1 What is cerebral palsy? How does it affect communication?

Activity 1

1. Observe a physically handicapped child who can talk with an adult.
   Can he talk like a child who is not physically handicapped?
   If not, why not?
   Write down three ways his talking is different.

2. Listen carefully to him.
   What is it about his speech that makes it hard to understand?
   Write down three reasons.

86

3. Does he know he is difficult to understand? Yes/No.
   Write down two reasons.

4. How does he help people to understand his speech?
   Write down three ways.

5. What other ways can you think of that would help him communicate so that people could understand his message?

Activity 2

1. Now observe a physically handicapped child who can't talk with an adult.
   How does he communicate?
   Write down at least four methods that he is using.

2. Is he showing frustration with his communication?
   How does he show his frustration?

3. What does he do when he is not understood?
   Give up? Yes/No
   Try again?
   Write down how he tries to make you understand.

Activity 3

How do adults communicate with:

- the physically handicapped child who cannot talk yet?
- the physically handicapped child who can talk but has speech problems?

Write down at least three things you observe, that are different, between the adult and the physically handicapped child who can't talk and the adult and the physically handicapped child who can talk.

Activity 4

Observe both these children again.

- Do you think because they have difficulties talking and communicating that they are stupid? Yes/No.
- Write down at least four things you have noticed about them during your observation that support your answer.

SECTION 4.2

How can we help cerebral palsied children with feeding problems?

Normal feeding development

When children are born they have a sucking reflex. Their tongue thrusts forward and then pulls back. These movements allow the young child to suck liquids. The child has to be held in a suitable position and has no head control.

Feeding development is a process of the child gaining voluntary control over this reflex behaviour. During the first 2 years of life, the child's feeding pattern develops from the basic sucking reflex to a mature pattern of chewing and swallowing.

To develop these mature feeding patterns the child needs to progress from just feeding on liquids to semi-solids like mashed banana or cereals and finally on to lumpy foods of different textures, and tastes.

Between 3 and 6 months the tongue stops thrusting forward so much and the lips take more part in sucking. This is when weaning and spoon feeding of semi-solids often begins. The child now has head control and is beginning to sit up.

Between 6 and 8 months the child becomes a much more efficient feeder. He learns to take food off a spoon by sucking it off with his top lip. He learns to drink from a cup. His lips are forming a good seal and his tongue is moving food to the back of his mouth for swallowing. He can be seen to chew up and down.

Between 8 months and 2 years, he gets teeth and learns to chew up and down first and then round and round as if he is chewing gum. During chewing both lips and teeth make seals for keeping the food in the mouth and for swallowing. Children need to practise chewing, so they must be given tough food they can chew.

Chewing encourages tongue tip movements which are very important for developing spoken language.

Feeding in cerebral palsied children

Feeding difficulties in this group of children are caused by lack of muscle control and co-ordination. Cerebral palsied children often have poor posture and lack of head control. They also often have limited movements and control over their tongue, lips and jaw.

Position

Putting the child in a good position for feeding is the first thing to do. The best way to achieve this is to try out different positions. Remember that:

1. The position should be comfortable for you and the child.
2. You need to be able to help the child, so you will probably need your hands free.
3. The child needs to be in a functional position – free enough to try to control his movements, particularly around his mouth and tongue but he needs to feel safe and secure, so he can concentrate on feeding and not worry about falling over. He should be as upright as possible. It is impossible to close your lips and swallow if your head is back and your neck stretched.

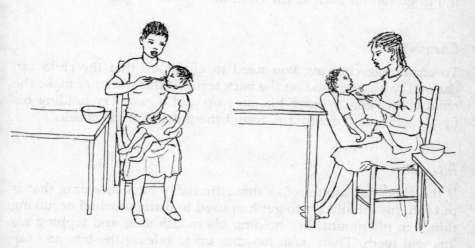

Good positions for feeding children with cerebral palsy

If the child has poor head control, support his head with your hand, so that his head is straight and his chin is up.

Do not force the child to open his mouth, suck or eat and drink anything he is firmly refusing.

You should encourage him to progress through the stages as naturally as possible.

Get the position right and ensure that the child is getting enough nourishment from the food. this will help him and make you feel more relaxed.

Poor sucking

If the child is very poor at sucking you could try stimulating the sucking reflex by rubbing something sweet and pleasant round his gums and over the tongue. Honey is good for this as it does not immediately run off. When you put the bottle in his mouth, try pressing gently under his chin. This will push the teat up against the roof of his mouth and squeeze the milk out. This should stimulate sucking. If this fails, you may have to spoon feed.

Tongue thrust

If the child has a tongue thrust (the tongue uncontrollably coming forward too much), try putting the food in the side of the mouth or in the middle of the tongue. If you put the food in the middle of the tongue, press down and back gently as you do it. Be careful not to go too far back as the child may choke or gag.

Chewing

To encourage chewing you need to give food that the child can chew. Try placing food on the back teeth. If this does not make the child chew, gently move his jaws up and down. Try holding his lips together and gently rub round the outside of his cheeks.

Bite reflex

If the child has a bite reflex (uncontrollably bites anything that is put into his mouth) try to get him used to being touched or having things in his mouth. Try holding his mouth shut and tapping his lips and teeth. Then push his chin up to release the bite and tap while his mouth is open.

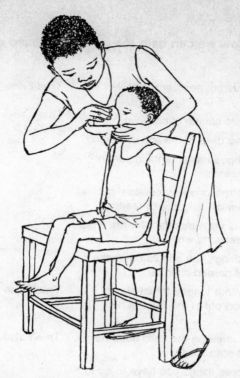

A good position for drinking from a cup for the cerebral palsied child

Drinking

Help the child to drink from a cup by controlling his head and keeping his chin up. Put your hand under his chin – this is probably easier to do if you are behind the child. Make sure the tongue is down and the cup rim is over the lower lip and teeth. Give the child a small amount of liquid and then remove the cup and push the lower lip up and the upper lip down to prevent the liquid falling out of the mouth. This makes a seal for swallowing.

REMEMBER IF YOU ARE WORRIED ABOUT FEEDING OR CROSS BECAUSE THE CHILD WILL NOT FEED, THE CHILD WILL KNOW HOW YOU ARE FEELING, AND HE WILL BECOME WORRIED, TENSE AND CROSS. THIS WILL RESULT IN AN UNHAPPY AND UNSUCCESSFUL FEEDING TIME FOR BOTH PARENT AND CHILD.

Questions

Section 4.2 How we can help the cerebral palsied child with feeding problems

1. Feeding does not need any muscle control.   True/False   **Marks:** 1

2. Name the two stages of chewing.   **Marks:** 2

3. What are two uses of the lips in feeding?   **Marks:** 2

4. Why are tongue movements important? Give two reasons.   **Marks:** 2

5. Name three reasons why cerebral palsied children have difficulties with feeding.   **Marks:** 3

6. Positioning is very important for the child. Give three reasons why.   **Marks:** 3

7. Name two things you should not make the cerebral palsied child do.   **Marks:** 2

8. The child with a tongue thrust should have the food put at the front of his mouth.   True/False   **Marks:** 1

9. To develop chewing the child does not need to eat solid food.   True/False   **Marks:** 1

10. What are three things you have to do to help the child drink from a cup.   **Marks:** 3

Skills

Section 4.2 How can we help the cerebral palsied child with feeding problems?

Activity 1

Observe a cerebral palsied child and help his parents to find a good feeding position for him. Do this by trying out different positions. Remember that:
- It has to be comfortable for the child and parent.
- The child has to be functional (able to do things) but also feel secure and supported.

Try each position out for more than one meal, observe the feeding time and then ask the parent what they felt about it. You and the parent should be able to find a position that is good for the child and the parent.

Try this activity with a number of cerebral palsied children. You will find that they are all different and their needs are different.

Activity 2

Help a parent wean her cerebral palsied child. Discuss with the parent how she will do this. Remember that she will probably be worried that her child will not get enough nourishment and might choke. You might consider:

- what sort of food to start the child on,
- how many feeds to change from liquid to semi-solids,
- what position to encourage the parent to use when feeding.

Activity 3

Write a programme for encouraging a child of 5 years to start eating solids and learning to chew. The child does not like lumpy food and the parents are worried the child will choke. You might like to consider:

- type of food,
- amount of food,
- rewards for changing his behaviour,
- physical problems with eating,
- behavioural problems with eating, or
- task analysis.

SECTION 4.3

How can we help a cerebral palsied child develop communication?

The cerebral palsied child needs to have a means of communicating, just like 'normal' children. There are a number of different ways he can do this:

- by making noises,
- by talking,
- by using gestures,
- by using sign language, e.g. Makaton,
- by using sign language that he has developed for himself,
- by eye pointing,
- by using a picture board,
- by using a word board, and,
- **by using a combination of these methods**.

The best communicators use lots of different ways to communicate. Learn to recognise the signals your child is giving out.

Saying Yes and No

One of the most useful communication skills that a cerebral palsied child can have is being able to indicate 'Yes' and 'No'.

If he can do this people around him can ask him lots of questions and by the child replying 'yes' or 'no' can gradually find out what the child wants or wants to communicate. Examples of ways in which he could do this, if he can't talk, are:

1. using his eyes, look up for 'Yes' and down for 'No';
2. using an arm movement, or a hand movement or a leg movement;
3. using two different noises or grunts;

4. facial expression – smiles for 'Yes' and looking sad and down for 'No'.

It doesn't matter what the movement is, as long as it is easy for the child to do and easily understandable to everybody around him.

Attracting attention

The child who cannot talk needs to be able to attract the attention of people when he wants to communicate something. If he can't do this, he is totally reliant on people noticing him or talking to him. This makes him very **passive** and means he only **responds** and does not **initiate**.

Anything to attract attention can be used, e.g. a bell, a rattle, a tin of stones to knock over, a particular grunt he makes, but everybody must understand that it means 'Listen I have something to say' and respond immediately by listening.

A cerebral palsied child ready to communicate

Time

Give the child **time** to communicate – because of his physical handicap it will take him much longer to express his message. He still needs you to respond, so you must look interested and wait for him to finish communicating. Try not to help him out by finishing the sentence for him. It is much better if he succeeds himself. It will encourage him to try again.

Questions

Section 4.3   Helping the cerebral palsied child to communicate

1.	Suggest six different ways that a cerebral palsied child who does not talk could indicate Yes and No.		**Marks:** 6
2.	Name four different ways that a cerebral palsied child who does not talk could attract attention.		**Marks:** 4
3.	The child may have difficulty in being noticed if he does not have something to attract attention.	True/False	**Marks:** 1
4.	The child is passive if he initiates communication.	True/False	**Marks:** 1
5.	Name four communicative functions that the child who does not talk can use.		**Marks:** 4
6.	These children need talking to all the time.	True/False	**Marks:** 1
7.	Give three reasons why the child who does not talk needs a method of communication.		**Marks:** 3

Skills

Section 4.3   Helping the cerebral palsied child to communicate

Activity 1

1. Observe a physically handicapped child who has some speech, but is hard to understand.
2. Suggest ways, i.e. other ways of communicating, that might help him to communicate.
3. Now help him or his family or his teacher, or all of them to **develop** other means of communication.
   - What will the child have to do?
   - What will his family and teachers have to do?

Activity 2

1. Observe a physically handicapped child who does not talk at all, i.e., he is non-verbal.
2. Write down the methods he is using for communication. See Section 4.3 page 94.
3. Can these methods be expanded? e.g. if he is using gestures, can you help him expand the number of gestures he is using and the use he is making of them. Could he for example combine two of his existing gestures to make a new one.
4. Would it help to introduce a completely new method of communicating? e.g. a picture or word board.
5. With the child, his parents and teachers design a communication board which will be **useful** to the child and help him expand the communication he is already using. See illustration of communication board on page 85.

Activity 3

Train the child and his parents and teachers to use all the methods of communication including the new ones you are introducing or the old ones you are trying to expand.
   Do not try and stop him using ways of communication because you think new ways are better, always build on what he's got and expand.
   Try this training programme on both the child who can talk a bit and the non-verbal child.

1. Ask parents and teachers to observe the child and notice the different methods the child is using to communicate.
2. Ask parents to observe the teacher communicating with the child and the teacher to observe the parent communicating with the child. **Points to note**:

a. Are parents and teachers responding to what the child is communicating?

b. Are parents and teachers asking lots of questions that just require a 'yes' or 'no', or are they asking 'open' questions that give the child a chance to express something, e.g. 'How did school go today?' or 'What would you like to do?'

c. Are parents and teachers leaving time for the child to respond and initiate conversation or are they talking so much there is no room?

d. Are parents and teachers having a conversation with the child or are they talking at the child and replying for him?

e. Are they using lots of different methods of communication?

f. Are they noticing all the communication signs the child is trying to use and responding to them?

3. Discuss the results of the observation with them and suggest ways in which they could change their communication with the child that would encourage the child to communicate more.

a. Use open questions (ones that cannot be answered with 'yes' or 'no'.

b. Respond to what the child says, both in time and content.

c. Leave **time** for the child to communicate.

d. Recognise all the communication signs the child is giving out. Encourage discussion of this between the teacher and the parent and you. You will probably notice different things.

e. Encourage new and expanded methods of communication to be included.

f. Talk to the child about new experiences he has so that he has the language to communicate about new things.

g. Always respond if the child has attracted your attention and wants to communicate.

4. Even though parents and teachers can communicate without making a lot of use of signs, gestures or picture boards, it is a good idea to encourage them to use these other methods with the child as it helps the child realise that these methods are just as good as talking. In addition to these, methods of communication that you can see, help the child to understand as they don't disappear as quickly as talking does.

PART 5

Spreading the Word

When you have read this book, have worked through the questions and have discussed the skills exercises with your friend and tried out the exercises, you will know quite a lot about communication and about the difficulties which mentally handicapped, deaf or cerebral palsied children have in learning to communicate with us.

You, as a health worker or CBR worker are used to working with people with disabilities. Many people in the community are frightened of people with disabilities and may not want to spend time with them or want to talk to them.

There is not a lot of point in us trying to help disabled children and their families to communicate better if the people in the community are not willing to talk to them. One of the CBR worker's jobs must be to help people in the village or community to understand disabled people better, not be frightened of them and to be prepared to talk to them. How can the CBR worker do this?

The first task must be for the CBR worker to convince the village and/or community that there is nothing to fear from these disabled children who sound funny when they try to talk. If the leaders, the religious leader, the teacher and others in authority accept these people's 'funny talking' then so too will other people in the community.

Perhaps the CBR worker could arrange to be invited to speak to church groups, to the men's group, to the mothers at the Health Centre or to any group where he/she can talk to adults who are not themselves parents of disabled children.

Perhaps she could get some school children to help him/her to make some simple posters. Posters which tell a very simple message e.g. 'speak clearly', 'look at my communication board', 'look at me when you talk to me', 'say things in simple words to me', 'give me lots of time to reply to you' etc.

Perhaps the CBR worker could make a simple leaflet to be given out at the health centre, e.g. about feeding in cerebral palsy, about talking to deaf children, about communication boards.

The CBR worker may find that some of the National Charities have leaflets or posters which she can use to spread the word about communication disorder.

Perhaps the CBR worker could get some of the able children to play a game seeing what it is like not to understand, or not to hear or not to talk. If children understand a little of the problem they are less likely to tease the disabled child.

One important thing which a CBR worker can do is to let the local newspaper or local radio know of something that one of the disabled children in his/her community or village has done well.

A poster giving simple information about hearing loss and where to go for help

The newspaper or radio may well publish the information and the more ordinary people hear of the achievements of disabled people the less mistrust there will be.

Anything that helps other people to understand the problems of disabled children who cannot communicate easily is going to make those disabled children less isolated within their communities.

PART 6
Where to Find Out More

1. In your country there is probably:
   - a National Association for Deaf People
   - a National Association for Cerebral Palsy
   - a National Association for Mental Handicap
   all of these will have useful leaflets, booklets etc.

2. Cerebral Palsy Overseas,
   6, Dukes Mews, London W1M 5RB, UK

   They have a useful quarterly magazine called *Interlink*

3. Commonwealth Society for the Deaf
   Dilke House, Malet Street
   London WC1 7JA, UK

4. AHRTAG (Appropriate Health Resource & Technologies Group)
   1, London Bridge St
   London SE1 9SG, UK

   They have a useful international newsletter called *CBR News*.

5. IDEA (International Disability Education & Awareness)
   William House
   101 Eden Vale Road
   Westbury, Wiltsire BA13 3QF, UK

6. TALC (Teaching Aids at Low Cost)
   PO Box 49, St Albans,
   Hertfordshire AL1 4AX, UK

7. Makaton Development Vocabulary Project
   31 Firwood Drive, Camberley, Surrey, UK

   For information about signs for disabled people.

8. There may be NGOs (non-governmental organisations) working in your area. They may be national or from overseas. Make contact with the NGOs and see what information they have to help you.

Answers and Comments

Answers to questions

ANSWERS to Section 1.1

1. False
2. False
3. True
4. (a)
5. (4) speech, spoken language, writing, reading, gestures, body language, facial expression, eye pointing, signs, finger spelling.
6. a) spoken language, vocalisation, speech
   b) gesture, body language, eye pointing, facial expression, signs, finger spelling.
7. questions, answering, responding, greeting, expressing ideas, expressing emotions.
8. rules, sounds, voice, words, messages, intonation, writing.
9. True
10. False

ANSWERS to Section 1.2

1. False
2. (3) gesture, touch, facial expression, body language, talking, singing
3. (3) gesture, smiling, vocalising, looking, wriggling
4. True
5. (4) imitation, repetition, exploring, asking, watching, seeing, hearing, touching
6. False
7. True
8. True
9. True
10. True
11. False
12. False
13. False

ANSWERS to Section 1.3

1. False
2. False
3. False
4. True
5. False (he will use two or three word combinations before sentences)
6. looking at the person or object being referred to
7. True
8. False

9. False (we should observe both but not forget input)
10. False (deaf children will not)
11. (4) eye pointing, facial expression, pointing, head turning, gestures
12. (4) carries out instructions, asks for information, likes stories, can fetch something, does not become bored with speech
13. False
14. False

ANSWERS to Section 1.4

1. False
2. False
3. True (blind children do learn to communicate but can have difficulties)
4. True
5. False
6. False
7. (4) cerebral palsy, mental handicap, deafness, structural problems, brain damage, brain disfunction.
8. hearing loss, cleft palate, injury to the face, stuttering, brain injury
9. False (listening is very important)
10. False
11. False
12. (c)
13. False
14. False

ANSWERS to Section 2.1

1. (c)
2. Decibels (db)
3. outer, middle and inner
4. middle, inner
5. between the outer and middle ear
6. by transfer of movement by the three little bones
7. conversion of sound to nervous impulses, transfer of impulses to brain
8. brain via hearing nerve
9. infection, puss, immobility of the little bones
10. False
11. True
12. (a)
13. False
14. (b)
15. False
16. True
17. False (except in very specialist centres)

ANSWERS to Section 2.2

1. False
2. False
3. False
4. False
5. False
6. False
7. False
8. anxiety, overprotection, denial

9. (3) partial, slight, moderate, severe, transient,
10. False
11. where there is infection or disease of the middle ear when the child has earache
12. (3) he scratches his ears,   he has throat infections
    he has earache   he does not listen
    he has coughs and colds   he is sometimes inattentive
13. False
14. (3) he behaves like a younger child
    he does not play with other children
    he is naughty or disruptive
    he is isolated (plays on his own)
    he is not popular

ANSWERS to Section 2.3

1. False
2. (3) signs, gestures, facial expression, speech, spoken language, finger spelling
3. (3) asking, confirming, greeting, telling
4. (c)
5. False
6. False
7. True
8. False
9. True
10. (2) Mummy, bye bye, water, 'moo' other easy words beginning with 'm' 'b' 'p' 'w'
11. False
12. False
13. True
14. False
15. False

ANSWERS to Section 3.1

1. False
2. False
3. True
4. True
5. (3) imitation, asking, curiosity, exploring, playing, doing
6. False (they will not learn more complex activities like driving a car)
7. (4) small steps, logical progress, rewards (reinforcers), meaningful, appropriate difficulty, usefulness
8. False
9. (4) meaningful target skill, broken into small steps, appropriate to child's level, structured teaching of skill, giving feeling of success, possible for parents to do, useful
10. (3) language, thinking, talking, reading, writing, numbers, fine motor movements

ANSWERS to Section 3.2

1. True
2. (3) attend, hear, listen, understand, decide what to say, say it
3. (5) use short sentences, use simple words, emphasise main words, speak slowly, plenty of space for child's reply, louder voice
4. False
5. False
6. False

108

7. (3) modelling, reinforcing, expanding, developing,
8. False
9. False
10. False (he should have some say in determining what words to use)
11. (2) talk at their level of input, use their interests, use complex sentences with adults, simple sentences with children

ANSWERS to Section 3.3

1. (4) watching, eye contact, turn-taking, listening, reaching, exploring
2. False
3. (3) singing, looking at books, talking to child as you work
4. False
5. (3) copying, real life activities, turn taking games, rhymes, animal noises
6. False
7. (3) singing, rhymes, playing
8. (4) responding, acknowledging, greeting, questioning, expanding

ANSWERS to Section 4.1

1. False
2. True
3. False
4. True
5. (5) vision, speech, movement, hearing, cognition, touch
6. False
7. (3) tongue, voice, lips, voice box, face, neck
8. False
9. (5) pointing, gesture, facial expression, sign, eyes, symbol boards
10. False (? understanding of learning difficulties)

ANSWERS to Section 4.2

1. False
2. up and down, round and round
3. (2) hold food in the mouth, hold the nipple, take food off the spoon, lip seal
4. (2) move food in the mouth, start to swallow, movements for speech
5. (3) poor co-ordination of head control, poor posture, muscle weakness, spacticity, limited movements
6. (3) comfortable, head erect, confidence, breathing, secure, able to swallow
7. open mouth if it is not easy to do so, eat or drink anything he is refusing
8. False
9. False
10. (3) positioning, keep chin up, control head, help form seal with lips around cup, (tongue down with lower lip under the rim)

ANSWERS to Section 4.3

1. eyes looking up and down, gestures, controlled arm movements, controlled hand movements, noises, word approximations
2. noises, tin of stones, rattle, bell
3. True
4. False
5. (4) greeting, asking, yes/no, initiating, responding
6. False
7. (3) avoid isolation, stimulate initiative, express needs, express emotions

Comments on skills

Section 1.1

Activity 1

1. Have you thought about:
   - spoken language?
   - crying and frowning?
   - smiling and laughing?
   - looking at each other? (Section 1.1 page 2)
   - written language?
   - pictures?
   - sounds?

2. and 3. The people will probably **not** be using all the communicative methods listed in Section 1.1 page 2.

4. This list will also include some of the communicative functions from Section 1.1 page 2, e.g.:

Listening
- eye contact
- watching
- attending
- concentrating
- responding
- looking at the person
- reading

Expressing
- spoken language
- smiling
- laughing
- frowning
- gesturing
- writing

Activity 2

Check from the lists above.

Activity 3

- greeting
- asking
- telling
- sharing information
- sharing emotion
- describing

The lists are the same for the adult and the child. See section 1.1 page 2.

Section 1.2

Activity 1

1. Have you included:
   - looking
   - smiling
   - listening
   - gurgling
   - waving arms and legs
   - making noises etc.

110

2. Have you included:
   - looking
   - singing
   - smiling
   - rocking
   - talking
   - touching etc.

4. Have you included:
   - copying mother movements or sounds
   - reaching for the mother
   - crying without great distress.

Activity 2

1. Have you thought about how many ideas the sentence has got? See section 1.2 page 12.

2. Have you thought about asking the child to:
   - give you 'more'
   - give you three plates from a pile of five
   - give you the 'big' stick from several of different sizes
   - give you the 'long' pencil from three
   - give you the 'red' flower from a choice of red/yellow.

4. See the communicative functions listed in Section 1.1

Activity 3

1. See comments above for the younger child

2. Have you thought about:
   - asking him to follow simple instructions
   - asking him to follow complicated instructions
   - asking to remember and then repeat a short list
   - asking him to give a simple message to someone
   - asking him to give a complex message to someone.

Section 1.4

Activity 1

1. Have you thought about:
   - listening
   - looking at each other
   - making noises
   - leaving space for each other
   - touching each other
   - reaching for each other.

Have you looked at who is initiating and who is responding?
   The initiator will control the interaction.

Activity 2

1. Look at who initiates (does the baby ever initiate?).
   Look at whether the mother talks a great deal.

2. Leave space for the baby to initiate.
   Look and listen to the baby's signals even if they are slow.

Activity 3

3. Have you thought about:
   - speaking more clearly
   - using gestures and spoken language
   - using shorter sentences.

Section 4.1

Activity 1

1. Have you thought about:
    - speed of speech
    - clarity of speech
    - amount of speech
    - lack of facial expression
    - his very short sentences
    - that he does not attend well.

2. Have you thought about:
    - the fact that his breathing is in short bursts
    - that his voice is not very loud
    - that his speech sounds are not clear or not all pronounced clearly (perhaps he misses the ends of words)
    - his intonation (the up and down of speech) is disturbed.

3. Because:
    - they do not listen to him
    - they do not answer him
    - he has become withdrawn (because people do not understand him)
    - he has given up trying
    - he has become very naughty.

4. He uses:
    - gestures
    - facial expression
    - eye contact
    - pointing.

5. Use:
    - a communication board
    - signs which have been developed for him
    - pointing
    - eye pointing.

Activity 2

1. - noises
    - arm and leg movements
    - head turning
    - pointing
    - reaching
    - eye pointing

2. Have you thought about:
    - understanding language
    - hearing language
    - vision
    - general learning difficulties (mental handicap).

Activity 3

Have you thought about:

a child who can talk
- slowly
- simply
- leave him too little space
- finish off what the child says
- do things for him.

a child who cannot talk
- less than usual
- using their hands
- give up and not talk
- ignore the child.

Activity 4

Have you thought about:
- general learning difficulties (slow milestones)

112

- understanding of language
- things to talk about
- having people to talk to
- being involved in the family.

Section 4.2

Activity 2

Have you thought about:
- porridge
- soup
- mashed banana
- mashed vegetables,

not
- hard things e.g. biscuits which will break in the child's mouth
- things with skins e.g. peas, corn
- things that need chewing a lot, e.g. meat.

Do not change all meals at once or the child will starve.

Start some feeds with semi-solids and then make sure he has enough nutrition with easier foods.

Section 4.3

Activity 1

Have you thought:
- that the child should use other methods of communication
- the child should listen carefully
- the child should not give up easily
- the adults should leave time
- the adults should use other methods of communication with their speech
- the adults must recognise messages that the child gives
- the adult must give opportunities for the child to express himself.

Index

attending 23
attending together 70–1, 76
attracting attention 95

babies, communication by 3, 8–11
bite reflex 90
blindness, and interaction skills 22
breathing, and cerebral palsy 84

CBR News 104
Cerebral Palsy Overseas 104
cerebral palsy 84
chewing 90
chewing development 88–9
communication vii, 13
    and cerebral palsy 85, 94, 97–8
    reasons for 2
    as two-way process 3, 8
communication development
    and deaf child 38–40
    mentally handicapped 60–1
communication initiation 16, 23
    by cerebral palsied 95
communication skills, and school
    attendance 46, 47, 80
communicative functions 2–3
    for deaf child 39
communicative methods 2
    of deaf child 39
conductive deafness 31

db (decibel) 29
Deaf, Society for 104
deafness
    causes 31, 33–4
    and interaction skills 22

and isolation 34
    observation for 35
decibel (db) 29
development of mentally
    handicapped 56–7
disruptive behaviour 46, 47
doctors viii
drinking, and cerebral palsy 91
dumbness 38

ear, anatomy 29–30
ear drum 29
ear infection 31, 33–4
ear mould 52, 53

fear, and the disabled 100
feeding children with cerebral palsy
    89–90
feeding development 88
frequency of sound 28
frustration 3
    in deaf child 39

generalisations of words 12
gestures, and mentally handicapped
    73
guilt, and deafness 34, 35

hearing aid 40, 50–1
    looking after 53
    problems with 52
hearing loss: see deafness

imitation, and mentally handicapped
    71, 76–7
infection of middle ear 31, 34

114